MACHINE LEARNING WITH RUST

A practical attempt to explore Rust and its libraries across popular machine learning techniques

Keiko Nakamura

GitforGits®
ASIAN PUBLISHING HOUSE

Published by: GitforGits

Publisher: Sonal Dhandre

www.gitforgits.com

support@gitforgits.com

Printed in India

First Printing: January 2024

ISBN: 9788119177936

Cover Design by: Kitten Publishing

Prologue

Prior to starting this writing expedition, I had a clear but challenging objective: to discover how the language Rust, which is known for being fast and safe, can work with the constantly changing field of machine learning. This book was written out of a mix of interest and a strong desire to go where no one has gone before, mapping out the places where Rust and machine learning meet. It's more of an exploration and story of finding than a claim to mastery. As the author, I'm not inviting you on this journey as a perfect teacher, but as a fellow learner eager to find out what can be done by combining the strength of Rust with the flexibility of machine learning methods.

It was important to make it clear from the start that this book is not meant to be the only way to learn machine learning with Rust. It's more of a starting point or introduction for people who are interested in what Rust can do for machine learning projects. Sharing knowledge and trying new things is what these pages are all about. The goal is to get you interested and give you a base from which to build.

We start with the basics and show you how Rust works so that even people who are new to the language can see what it can do. The steps in the book are similar to how I learned Rust: from getting to know its syntax and features to looking into how its ideas can be used to make machine learning methods work better, they are similar.

The exploring spirit of this book stays true as we learn about different machine learning techniques, from basic algorithms to more complex neural networks. The datasets of COVID, CIFAR-10 and practical examples are meant to show the way by showing how Rust's features, such as its speed, memory safety, and concurrency, can be used to deal with the problems that come up in machine learning projects.

The main idea of this book is to ask questions, learn, and discover what hasn't been explored before. Developers and experts alike think that combining Rust and machine learning can lead to new discoveries. Although there are technical details, the story does not present them as a declaration of knowledge. Instead, it does so as a conversation, encouraging you to try new things, dig deeper, and help us learn more.

Finally, I want to recommend this book to anyone who is interested in what can happen when Rust and machine learning come together. It opens the door to new ideas by showing how the rules of a systems programming language can be combined with machine learning to encourage new ideas. As we turn the pages together, let's start this journey with an open mind and a desire to learn, ready to discover the huge possibilities that lie ahead. At any point, you encounter correction, please do not forget to highlight them up to us at support@gitforgits.com

Content

Preface

In this stimulating book, you'll learn how to use the Rust programming language in conjunction with machine learning. It's not a full guide to learning machine learning with Rust. Instead, it's more of a journey that shows you what's possible when you use Rust to solve machine learning problems. Some people like Rust because it is quick and safe. This book shows how those qualities can help machine learning a lot.

To begin, we will show you what Rust is and how it works. This is so that everyone, even those who are new to Rust, can follow along. Then, we look at some basic machine learning concepts, such as linear and logistic regression, and show how to use Rust's tools and libraries to make these ideas work.

You will learn more complex techniques like decision trees, support vector machines, and how to work with data as we go along. It goes all the way up to neural networks and image recognition, and we show you how to use Rust for these types of tasks step by step. We use real-world examples, such as COVID data and the CIFAR-10 image set, to show how Rust works with issues that come up in the real world.

This book is all about discovery and experimentation. To see what you can do with them, we use various Rust tools for machine learning. It's a fun way to see how Rust can be used in machine learning, and it will make you want to try new things and learn more on your own. This is only the beginning; there is so much more to uncover as you continue to explore machine learning with Rust.

In this book you will learn how to:

- Exploit Rust's efficiency and safety to construct fast machine learning models.
- Use Rust's ndarray crate for numerical computations to manipulate complex machine learning data.
- Find out how Rust's extensible machine learning framework, linfa, works across algorithms to comprehend the ecosystem.
- Use Rust's precision and speed to construct linear and logistic regression.
- See how Rust crates simplify decision trees and random forests for prediction and categorization.
- Learn to implement and optimize probabilistic classifiers, SVMs and closest neighbor methods in Rust.
- Use Rust's computing power to study neural networks and CNNs for picture recognition and processing.

- Apply learnt strategies to COVID and CIFAR-10 datasets to address realistic problems and obtain insights.

GitforGits

Prerequisites

This book is for aspiring Rust programmers, newbies to machine learning, and to machine learning professionals who want to witness the possibilities of Rust in machine learning. The book just expects you to be eager to explore Rust in machine learning and no other thing is desired to pull this book.

Codes Usage

Are you in need of some helpful code examples to assist you in your programming and documentation? Look no further! Our book offers a wealth of supplemental material, including code examples and exercises.

Not only is this book here to aid you in getting your job done, but you have our permission to use the example code in your programs and documentation. However, please note that if you are reproducing a significant portion of the code, we do require you to contact us for permission.

But don't worry, using several chunks of code from this book in your program or answering a question by citing our book and quoting example code does not require permission. But if you do choose to give credit, an attribution typically includes the title, author, publisher, and ISBN. For example, "Machine Learning with Rust by Keiko Nakamura".

If you are unsure whether your intended use of the code examples falls under fair use or the permissions outlined above, please do not hesitate to reach out to us at support@gitforgits.com.

We are happy to assist and clarify any concerns.

Acknowledgement

I owe a tremendous debt of gratitude to GitforGits, for their unflagging enthusiasm and wise counsel throughout the entire process of writing this book. Their knowledge and careful editing helped make sure the piece was useful for people of all reading levels and comprehension skills. In addition, I'd like to thank everyone involved in the publishing process for their efforts in making this book a reality. Their efforts, from copyediting to advertising, made the project what it is today.

Finally, I'd like to express my gratitude to everyone who has shown me unconditional love and encouragement throughout my life. Their support was crucial to the completion of this book. I appreciate your help with this endeavour and your continued interest in my career.

CHAPTER 1: RUST BASICS FOR MACHINE LEARNING

Machine Learning Landscape

Over the last ten years, machine learning has become a very influential technology, significantly reshaping various industries. Machine learning models are being used for a wide range of applications, from automating routine work in offices to transforming healthcare diagnoses. Machine learning is pervasive even in our everyday activities. Netflix and Google Maps utilize machine learning models to provide recommendations and optimize routes, respectively. These algorithms utilize historical data to generate predictions or make judgments without requiring explicit programming. The ability to acquire knowledge, known as 'learning', has rendered machine learning essential for addressing intricate problems that cannot be effectively solved using conventional programming approaches.

Structure and Components of Machine Learning

Machine learning fundamentally revolves around the identification and extraction of patterns within datasets. The process commences with gathering a dataset that is pertinent to the current challenge. The data is subsequently partitioned into training and testing sets, with the former facilitating the algorithm's learning process and the latter assessing its success. Diverse methods, spanning from basic linear regression to intricate neural networks, are employed to construct models capable of predicting outcomes or classifying data. The precision of these models relies on the caliber of the data and the suitability of the algorithm employed. Machine learning is a field that constantly evolves as new data is incorporated into updated models. The dynamic and evolving nature of machine learning requires a programming environment that is both efficient and adaptable, which is where programming languages like Rust come into play.

Types of Machine Learning

Machine learning can be classified into three main types: Supervised Learning, which involves the model learning from labeled data to make predictions; Unsupervised Learning, which involves the model identifying patterns in unlabeled data; and Reinforcement Learning, which involves an agent learning how to perform actions in an environment to achieve a specific goal. These categories are not completely separate; numerous practical applications employ a combination of these methods. An example of this is a self-driving automobile, which employs supervised learning to recognize objects, unsupervised learning to comprehend road conditions, and reinforcement learning to navigate through traffic. The complex and varied nature of machine learning requires a programming language that can effectively handle a wide range of methods and enormous datasets. Rust is a highly suitable choice for this purpose.

Why Rust for ML?

The selection of a programming language for machine learning is crucial, and Rust distinguishes itself for various reasons. Rust is widely recognized for its memory safety features, which effectively eliminate numerous common errors and vulnerabilities during the compilation process.

This results in machine learning applications that are more secure. The performance of this language is on par with languages such as C and C++, providing the necessary computational speed for demanding machine learning tasks. The advanced type system and ownership model of Rust facilitate the development of concurrent code, a crucial requirement for machine learning algorithms that necessitate parallel execution. In addition, Rust's package manager, Cargo, streamlines dependency management, facilitating the integration of diverse machine learning libraries and frameworks.

Prospects of Machine Learning

The future of machine learning appears exceptionally promising as technological titans such as Google, Microsoft, and Amazon make substantial investments in this field. Currently, we are observing progress in technologies such as Generative Adversarial Networks (GANs) which are capable of generating realistic images, and Natural Language Processing (NLP) algorithms that possess the ability to write in a manner similar to humans. Machine learning models are currently employed in healthcare to achieve early disease diagnosis, resulting in significant enhancements in patient outcomes. Quantum Machine Learning is the upcoming domain in which machine learning algorithms will be executed on quantum computers, providing unparalleled speed and capability. These technical developments unequivocally indicate that machine learning will remain at the forefront of technological innovation. Therefore, now is an opportune moment to delve into this captivating topic.

Basics of Rust Programming

Memory Safety and Ownership

One of the most appealing aspects of Rust is its emphasis on memory safety while maintaining efficiency. Unlike languages such as Python or Java, which utilize a garbage collector to manage memory, or C and C++, which delegate this duty to the programmer, Rust has a unique ownership system with a set of rules that the compiler checks at compile time. The ownership mechanism assures that each value has a single 'owner,' and when the owner moves out of scope, the value is deallocated. This removes typical problems such as null pointer dereferencing, dangling pointers, and data races, improving the security and reliability of machine learning programs. For example, if we are developing a large-scale data analytics engine that demands multi-threading and low latency, Rust's ownership paradigm ensures that data is accessible securely and efficiently.

Concurrency

Another area where Rust excels is in concurrent programming. Data scientists and machine learning engineers frequently work with huge datasets that require parallel processing to save time and computational resources. Rust's ownership paradigm flows neatly into its concurrency model. Rust makes it impossible to incorporate data races and other concurrency-related issues into your code by maintaining a clear distinction between mutable and immutable references, which is enforced at compile-time. This is critical for machine learning methods such as Random Forest and Gradient Boosting, which benefit from parallel processing. To support concurrent programming, the language provides a variety of primitives such as threads, atomic operations, and channels. You may use these characteristics to create high-performance, concurrent code for your machine learning algorithms that is both fast and safe.

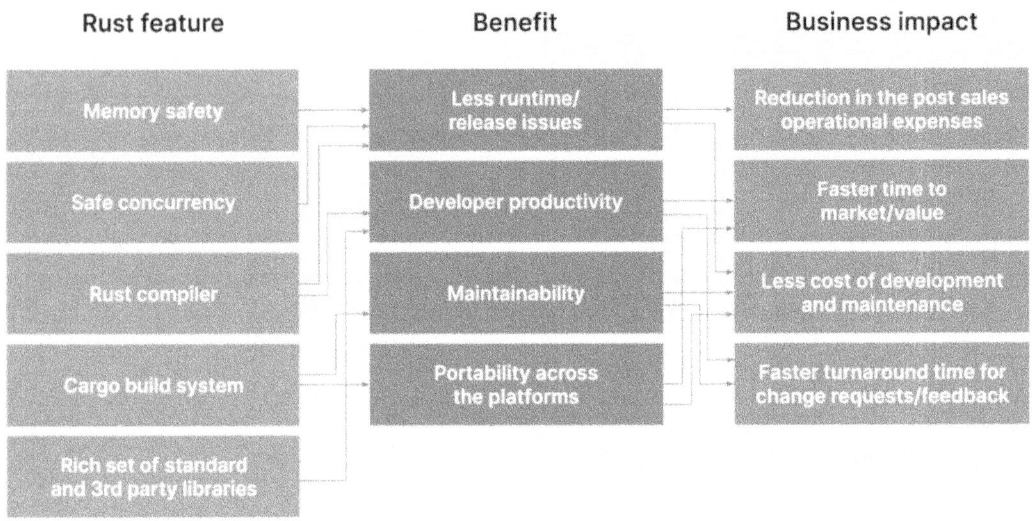

Fig 1.1 Features of Rust Language

Error Handling

When it comes to error management, Rust differs from many other programming languages. It does not use exceptions and instead includes two main types for handling errors: Option and Result. The Option type eliminates null-related concerns by allowing for values to be either something or nothing. The Result type is used for functions that may fail. T is the value returned in the event of success, while E is the error returned in the case of failure. This explicit technique requires you to handle errors, which makes your code more robust. This is especially useful in machine learning applications where data may be absent, distorted, or presented in an unexpected format. Instead of destroying your entire model training process, Rust's error-handling tools let you to detect and manage problems properly.

Comprehensive Ecosystem and Package Management

Cargo, Rust's package manager, is another advantage that makes it an excellent candidate for machine learning. Cargo manages project builds and retrieves the library dependencies specified in a simple configuration file. It's quite simple, allowing you to spend less time dealing with dependency concerns and more time working on your machine learning project. This is extremely useful because machine learning projects frequently require multiple specialized libraries for activities such as data manipulation, algorithm development, and model validation. The Rust ecosystem is quickly expanding, with various machine learning-specific libraries available, including 'linfa' for classical algorithms and 'tch-rs' for deep learning with Torch.

Interoperability with Different Languages

Rust can work seamlessly with C, allowing you to invoke C libraries and functions as if they were Rust functions. This is especially beneficial in the field of machine learning, since many high-performance libraries are built in C or C++. Rust's Foreign Function Interface (FFI) allows you to easily integrate existing libraries into your machine learning project. Suppose you have a machine learning model developed in another language, such as Python. In such an instance, you can wrap it in a Rust interface to improve performance and safety assurances, allowing for a more gradual transition to a fully Rust-based solution over time.

These basics should help you get started with using Rust for machine learning. The language's emphasis on performance, safety, and robustness makes it an appealing option for developing dependable, high-speed machine learning algorithms and applications.

Cargo and Popular Rust Packages

Cargo Overview

Cargo serves as a comprehensive tool for constructing, evaluating, and documenting Rust projects, surpassing its role as a mere package management. It simplifies various duties related to administering a Rust project, allowing developers to concentrate on coding instead of dealing with tedious build processes. When initiating a new project with Cargo, it automatically establishes a conventional directory framework and generates configuration files on your behalf. The declaration of all your dependencies is consolidated in a single Cargo.toml file, facilitating the comprehension and administration of your project's prerequisites. This is especially advantageous in machine learning projects where you may depend on many libraries for tasks such as data preprocessing, statistical modeling, and visualization. Integrating a new library with Cargo is a straightforward process where you just need to include a line in your Cargo.toml file and execute the cargo build command.

Managing Dependencies

Effectively handling dependencies in a project can be a challenging endeavor, however Cargo significantly streamlines this procedure. Within the realm of machine learning, your project may rely on libraries for the manipulation of data, execution of mathematical operations, and utilization of specialized machine learning algorithms. Cargo handles the tasks of downloading these dependencies, building them, and linking them to your project. Furthermore, it maintains a record of transitive dependencies, guaranteeing compatibility among all libraries. The automated process of resolving dependencies is a notable benefit, particularly when dealing with intricate machine learning applications that necessitate multiple specialized libraries. There is no need for you to manually download each library, verify its version, and resolve conflicts, as Cargo automates these processes effectively.

Cargo's Extensibility

Cargo is capable of being expanded or extended. The natural world Cargo is not solely confined to managing dependencies and performing builds; it is also very adaptable and allows for the use of custom commands. This is particularly advantageous for machine learning processes in which tasks such as data preprocessing, model training, and deployment may be required. By using custom Cargo commands, you can automate these procedures and seamlessly include your whole machine learning workflow into the Rust environment. This minimizes the burden of switching between different tasks and streamlines the process of creating software. These custom instructions can be shared between projects, facilitating the implementation of best practices and ensuring consistency in machine learning initiatives.

ndarray and ndarray-linalg

ndarray is a fundamental library that is used for numerical computing and machine learning. The library offers an n-dimensional array object that enables efficient and convenient manipulation of data. The API of ndarray-linalg is designed to be user-friendly and is strongly influenced by NumPy, a widely utilized library in the Python ecosystem. ndarray-linalg expands upon ndarray by incorporating linear algebra operations, which play a vital role in machine learning methods. These libraries are fundamental components used to construct different machine learning algorithms from the beginning or for performing data preprocessing tasks.

Linfa

linfa is a widely used package for machine learning. linfa strives to offer an extensive assortment of algorithms and tools for machine learning. The library includes implementations for a diverse range of machine learning methods, such as k-Means for clustering and logistic regression for classification, among others. The design of this system prioritizes efficiency and is constructed on the foundation of ndarray. This feature makes it an optimal selection for machine learning practitioners seeking to utilize Rust for comprehensive machine learning assignments. Linfa offers a diverse range of functionalities to support activities such as data preprocessing, feature extraction, and model training.

tch-rs and tract

Tch-rs is a Rust binding for PyTorch, designed specifically for individuals with a keen interest in deep learning. It enables you to utilize the capabilities and adaptability of PyTorch while benefiting from the efficiency and security attributes of Rust. By utilizing PyTorch for model development and testing, and subsequently deploying the model with Rust, the process of integrating deep learning models into production systems becomes more streamlined. Tract is a deep learning framework that specifically emphasizes the execution of pre-trained models. This software is specifically created to enhance productivity and may enhance models to fit a particular input structure, making it well-suited for real-time tasks such as natural language processing or picture identification in the Rust programming language.

The growing ecosystem of machine learning libraries and Cargo's strong package management are making Rust a more appealing choice for building ML applications. Its emphasis on efficiency, security, and user-friendliness renders it well-suited for individuals at all skill levels in the domain of machine learning.

Setting up Rust Environment

When developing machine learning applications, which make use of a wide variety of specialized libraries and tools, it is essential to first set up the Rust environment before beginning to code. In this section, we will go over the basics of installing Rust, organizing your development environment, and installing the necessary packages for numerical computation and machine learning.

Installing Rust and Cargo

The first step is to install the Rust programming language itself, along with its package manager, Cargo. Rust provides a straightforward installation process through a script that you can run in your terminal. You can install Rust by executing the command `curl --proto '=https' --tlsv1.2 -sSf https://sh.rustup.rs | sh`. This script downloads a number of components, including the `rustc` compiler, the `rustup` toolchain installer, and Cargo. After installation, you will have to add the Rust toolchain to your system's PATH. Usually, the installation script does this for you, but if not, you can add it manually. With Rust and Cargo installed, we are now equipped to create, build, and manage Rust projects. It's essential to verify the installation by running `rustc --version` and `cargo --version` to ensure that both are correctly installed.

Selecting IDE or Text Editor

Once Rust and Cargo are installed, the next step is to choose an IDE or a text editor that supports Rust development. There are several options available, such as Visual Studio Code with the Rust extension, IntelliJ IDEA with its Rust plugin, or even Vim or Emacs with Rust-specific configurations. Each of these options comes with features like syntax highlighting, code completion, and integrated terminal access, making it easier to write and debug Rust code. The choice of IDE is subjective and depends on your personal preference and the specific needs of your machine learning project. Some IDEs offer more advanced debugging and profiling features, which can be extremely useful when working with complex machine learning algorithms.

Initializing New Project

Creating a new Rust project is simplified with Cargo. Navigate to the directory where you want to create your project and run cargo new project_name, replacing project_name with the name you choose. This command sets up a new Rust project with a standard directory structure and a Cargo.toml file, where you will specify your project's dependencies. The src folder contains a main.rs file, which is the entry point of your application. With this structure, Cargo makes it easy to organize your code, resources, and dependencies, which is vital in machine learning projects that often consist of multiple modules and require various libraries.

Installing Essential Packages

For machine learning and numerical computing, several Rust packages (also known as crates) are commonly used. You can add these packages as dependencies in your Cargo.toml file. For instance, to include the ndarray crate for array computations, you would add ndarray = "0.15" under the [dependencies] section in Cargo.toml. Other essential crates like ndarray-linalg for linear algebra, linfa for machine learning algorithms, or tch-rs for deep learning can be added similarly. Once the dependencies are declared, running cargo build will download and compile these crates, making them available for use in your project. This is a crucial step as these libraries provide the building blocks for implementing machine learning algorithms and models.

Testing Environment with Simple Program

Before diving into complex machine learning algorithms, it is advisable to test your environment with a simple Rust program. Create a new file within the src directory, perhaps named simple_test.rs. Write a simple Rust function, maybe one that performs a basic array operation using the ndarray crate. You can then run this file using cargo run --bin simple_test to ensure that all dependencies are correctly installed and the environment is properly configured. This step ensures that you are ready to proceed with more complex tasks like data manipulation, feature extraction, and machine learning model implementation.

If everything goes according to plan, you should end up with a Rust environment that is perfect for numerical computation and machine learning. It is impossible to design and implement machine learning algorithms and applications without first laying this groundwork. Now that everything is set up, you can hop into Rust and see what it can do in the world of machine learning.

Structure Machine Learning Projects

The success of any machine learning project hinges on the establishment of a meticulously planned project structure. Code, data, and resources may be more easily managed and the development process can be streamlined with an organized and sensible folder structure.

Root Directory and Workspace Configuration

The root directory of your project should contain configuration files that are essential for building and running your project. This includes the Cargo.toml file, which specifies the project's dependencies and other configurations. It's also a good practice to include a README.md file to provide an overview of the project, its purpose, and how to get it up and running. You might also include a Makefile or a script for automating common tasks like data preprocessing, model training, and evaluation. For managing different versions of Rust or for setting environment variables, you can use a .env file or a tool like rustup override to set a specific Rust version for the project. This root directory serves as the central hub from which all other components emanate, so it should be as clean and self-explanatory as possible.

Source Code Organization

Inside the src/ directory, your Rust source code files reside. It's common to have a main.rs file as the project's entry point. However, for a machine learning project, it is often beneficial to modularize your code further. For instance, you might have subdirectories like data_preprocessing/, feature_extraction/, models/, and evaluation/. Each of these folders can contain Rust files pertinent to those aspects of machine learning. For example, data_preprocessing/ could contain Rust files that use the ndarray and ndarray-linalg crates for manipulating data. The models/ directory could leverage the linfa crate for implementing machine learning algorithms. This modular approach makes it easier to manage and extend your codebase.

Data Folder for Datasets and Resources

A data/ directory should be part of the project to store various datasets, whether they are raw data files or preprocessed ones. This folder might contain subdirectories like raw/ and processed/ to segregate the data further. It's essential to include a README.md file in this folder that explains the data's source, structure, and any preprocessing steps that have been or need to be taken. While the data folder is crucial for local development and testing, it is often omitted from version control systems by including it in the .gitignore file, especially if the data is large or sensitive.

Model Artifacts and Evaluation Metrics

Another crucial component is a directory to store trained machine learning models and their evaluation metrics, perhaps named artifacts/. This folder can have subdirectories like trained_models/ and evaluation_metrics/ to store serialized models and performance reports, respectively. These could be in the form of binary files, JSON, or even CSV files that log model performance over time. When you train a model using linfa or tch-rs, you will serialize the trained model parameters and save them in the trained_models/ directory. Similarly, any performance metrics, graphs, or logs generated during the model evaluation phase can reside in evaluation_metrics/.

Documentation and Notebooks

In a directory named docs/, you can keep project documentation, API references, and any design documents or specifications. For machine learning projects, it is also common to include Jupyter Notebooks or equivalent that contain exploratory data analysis, model experiments, or even tutorials on how to use the code. This can be particularly useful for educational projects like this book, where you might benefit from a more interactive way to engage with the material. You can include these notebooks in a subdirectory like notebooks/ within the docs/.

My First Rust Program

To become proficient in Rust, it is essential to write a basic program. Since you seem to be interested in practical uses of machine learning, we will go over a simple example that makes use of numerical operations and the ndarray library to manipulate arrays. As an added bonus, you will learn about a package that is commonly used.

Setting up Project Directory

Since you are using a text editor, navigate to the directory where you want to start your project. Create a new folder named simple_rust_program. Within this folder, create another folder named src. This is where all your Rust source code will reside. Next, create a file named Cargo.toml in the simple_rust_program directory. Open this file in your text editor and add the following content:

```
[package]

name = "simple_rust_program"

version = "0.1.0"

edition = "2018"



[dependencies]
```

```
ndarray = "0.15.4"
```

The Cargo.toml file defines the project metadata and dependencies. In this case, we're specifying a dependency on version 0.15.4 of the ndarray crate.

Creating Main Rust File

Next, navigate to the src folder you created and create a file named main.rs. This will be the entry point for your Rust program. The .rs extension is used for Rust source files. Open this main.rs file in your text editor to start writing your code.

Importing Library and Initializing Arrays

Start by importing the ndarray library and its Array module. Then, initialize two arrays that you will perform operations on. The code will look something like this:

```
extern crate ndarray;

use ndarray::Array;


fn main() {

 let array1 = Array::from_shape_vec((2, 2), vec![1., 2., 3., 4.]).unwrap();

 let array2 = Array::from_shape_vec((2, 2), vec![4., 3., 2., 1.]).unwrap();


 println!("Array 1:\n{:?}", array1);

 println!("Array 2:\n{:?}", array2);

}
```

In the above code snippet, we're using the from_shape_vec function from ndarray to create a 2x2 array. The unwrap() function is used to handle any errors that may arise from this operation. We then print out these arrays to the console.

Performing Array Operations

Now that you have initialized your arrays, we now perform some basic operations like addition and multiplication:

```
let sum = &array1 + &array2;

let product = &array1 * &array2;


println!("Sum of arrays:\n{:?}", sum);

println!("Element-wise product of arrays:\n{:?}", product);
```

In the above program, we're leveraging the **ndarray** library's overloaded operators for array operations. The **&** symbol is used to borrow the array, allowing the original arrays to be reused for other operations.

Running the Program

To compile and run your program, open your terminal, navigate to your **simple_rust_program** directory, and execute the command **cargo run**. This command does several things: it downloads the **ndarray** crate specified in your **Cargo.toml**, compiles your **main.rs** source file, and runs the resulting executable. You should see the initialized arrays, their sum, and element-wise product printed to the console. This simple program serves as an introduction to both basic Rust programming and numerical operations using the **ndarray** library.

Organizing Dependencies in Cargo.toml

One of the key features of Cargo is its ability to manage dependencies through the **Cargo.toml** file. You can categorize dependencies under different sections to make it easier to manage various aspects of your machine learning project. For instance, you could have a **[dependencies.ml]** section specifically for machine learning libraries like **linfa** or **tch-rs**, and another section **[dependencies.data]** for data manipulation libraries like **ndarray** or **ndarray-linalg**. This makes it easier to locate and manage dependencies related to specific tasks. Given below is a sample categorization in a **Cargo.toml** file:

```
[dependencies]

# General purpose libraries

serde = "1.0"
```

```
[dependencies.ml]

linfa = "0.3"

tch = "0.4"


[dependencies.data]

ndarray = "0.15"

ndarray-linalg = "0.13"
```

Creating Feature Flags

Rust and Cargo offer a powerful feature known as "features" that enable conditional compilation of parts of your codebase. This is useful in machine learning projects where you might want to switch between different algorithms or data processing techniques without altering the codebase. In the Cargo.toml, you can define features that enable specific dependencies or even modules within your project. For instance, if we are exploring both deep learning and classical algorithms, you can define features to conditionally include libraries like tch-rs or linfa:

```
[features]

deep-learning = ["tch"]

classical-ml = ["linfa"]
```

In your Rust code, you can then use #[cfg(feature = "deep-learning")] and #[cfg(feature = "classical-ml")] annotations to conditionally compile code based on the activated features.

Utilizing Dev and Build Dependencies

Cargo allows you to specify dependencies that are only used during development and testing or only during build time. This is specified under [dev-dependencies] and [build-dependencies] in your Cargo.toml. For instance, you may use a package like tempdir to create temporary directories during testing but don't need it in the final compiled program. This segregation keeps your production dependencies lean, ensuring that unnecessary packages don't make it into the final build.

[dev-dependencies]

tempdir = "0.3"

Versioning in Cargo

Managing package versions is crucial in ensuring that your project remains stable over time. Cargo provides several options to specify versions flexibly. You can lock to a specific version, specify a version range, or even use wildcard characters. For example, using ndarray = "0.15*" would mean any patch version that is compatible with 0.15 is acceptable. This allows you to maintain a balance between stability and receiving updates for the packages you use.

In more complex machine learning projects, you might find yourself working on multiple related packages simultaneously. For instance, you might have one package for data preprocessing, another for model training, and yet another for deployment. Cargo workspaces enable you to manage multiple related packages under a single Cargo.toml file. Each package will have its own Cargo.toml, but dependencies common to multiple packages can be specified in the workspace's Cargo.toml, preventing duplication and making management easier.

Rust IDEs

We dive into the JetBrains IDE specifically tailored for Rust development, known as IntelliJ Rust. While text editors are excellent for lightweight tasks and quick coding, an Integrated Development Environment (IDE) offers a more feature-rich platform that can significantly enhance productivity, especially for larger projects like those often encountered in machine learning. IntelliJ Rust brings the robustness of JetBrains IDEs to Rust programming, providing a suite of tools for code writing, debugging, and project management, all integrated into a single platform.

Why IntelliJ?

IntelliJ Rust offers several features that can accelerate your development process, making it a strong choice for machine learning projects. Some of the standout features include smart code completion, on-the-fly error checking with quick-fix suggestions, and powerful refactoring tools. The IDE also integrates seamlessly with Cargo, making dependency management and task automation straightforward. Another advantage is its debugging capabilities. You can debug Rust code just like you would in other languages, set breakpoints, and inspect variables, all within the IDE. It also supports unit testing out of the box, allowing you to write and run tests without leaving the IDE. These features make IntelliJ Rust an excellent tool for both new learners and experienced developers.

Downloading and Installing IntelliJ IDEA

To use IntelliJ Rust, you will first need to download IntelliJ IDEA, which is the base IDE that supports the Rust plugin. JetBrains offers two versions: the Ultimate version, which is paid but comes with additional features, and the Community version, which is free. For Linux, you can download the tar.gz archive from the official website. Once downloaded, extract it using `tar -xzf ideaIC-2021.2.3.tar.gz` (replace `ideaIC-2021.2.3.tar.gz` with the actual file name if different). After extraction, navigate to the `bin` directory inside the extracted folder and run the `idea.sh` script to start the IDE: `./idea.sh`.

Installing Rust Plugin

Once IntelliJ IDEA is up and running, navigate to File -> Settings (or IntelliJ IDEA -> Preferences on some Linux distributions) and then go to Plugins. In the marketplace tab, search for Rust and click Install. This will download and install the Rust plugin, adding all the Rust-specific features to IntelliJ IDEA. You will need to restart the IDE to complete the plugin installation.

Configuring IDE

After installing the Rust plugin, you will need to configure the IDE to recognize your Rust installation and Cargo settings. Go to File -> Settings -> Languages & Frameworks -> Rust, and here you can specify the location of your Rust toolchain and customize other settings like the format style. The IDE usually auto-detects the Rust installation if it is available in the system PATH. For Cargo integration, the IDE automatically reads your `Cargo.toml` and offers options for running and building your project right from the IDE interface.

Creating First Rust Project in IntelliJ

Creating a new Rust project is straightforward. Go to File -> New -> Project, choose Rust as the project type, and then configure the project's name and location. Once created, you will see that IntelliJ Rust automatically generates a project structure similar to what `cargo new` would produce, including a `Cargo.toml` file for dependencies and a `main.rs` file as the project's entry point. You can now start adding your code, and the IDE will assist you with code completion, error checking, and other smart features.

Debugging and Testing in IntelliJ

One of the strengths of using an IDE like IntelliJ Rust is the robust debugging and testing tools it offers. The debugging interface allows you to set breakpoints, step through code, and inspect variable states, providing a comprehensive debugging experience. For testing, IntelliJ Rust recognizes Rust's native test annotations and allows you to run individual tests or entire test suites directly from the IDE. These features are incredibly beneficial when we are developing complex machine learning algorithms where debugging and testing can become intricate.

With IntelliJ Rust set up on your Linux system, we are now equipped with a powerful tool that can significantly enhance your Rust programming experience, especially for complex tasks like machine learning projects. The IDE's integration with Cargo, along with its advanced coding, debugging, and testing features, offers a comprehensive development environment that can boost both your productivity and code quality.

Preparing ML Environment for Release

Releasing a Rust project involves a series of steps aimed at preparing your code for deployment or distribution. This includes optimizing your code for performance, managing dependencies, setting version numbers, and finally, packaging the compiled binaries and libraries. Given that we're working with a simple Rust program that performs array operations using the ndarray library, we now walk through the process of releasing this project.

Optimizing Code for Release

By default, Cargo builds your project in debug mode, which prioritizes compilation speed and includes debugging information at the cost of runtime performance. For a release, you will want to build in release mode by running cargo build --release. This command instructs Cargo to optimize your code for performance. Under the hood, Cargo uses the --release flag to enable higher optimization levels, remove debugging information, and set other compiler flags aimed at improving runtime efficiency. This is crucial for machine learning projects, where computational performance can significantly impact the usability and effectiveness of your algorithms or models.

Managing Dependencies and Updating Crates

Before releasing your project, it is good practice to update your dependencies. Run cargo update to fetch the latest compatible versions of your project's dependencies as per your Cargo.toml. This ensures that you are shipping your project with the latest security patches and performance improvements. However, be cautious when updating, as new versions can introduce breaking changes. It's advisable to run your test suite after updating to ensure that everything still works as expected.

Setting Version Number and Metadata

Versioning is crucial when releasing a project. Semantic versioning is commonly used in the Rust ecosystem, and you should specify the version of your project in the Cargo.toml under the [package] section. Additionally, ensure to include other metadata like the project description, authors, and license. This information is essential for both individual users and package managers to understand what your package does, who maintains it, and under what terms it can be used.

```
[package]

name = "simple_rust_program"

version = "1.0.0"

description = "A simple Rust program for array operations using ndarray"

authors = ["Your Name <youremail@example.com>"]

license = "MIT"
```

Creating Release Profile

Cargo allows you to customize build profiles in the `Cargo.toml` file. You can specify additional compiler flags or features for the release profile. For instance, you can further optimize the binary size or enable specific features only when building for release. This is done under the `[profile.release]` section in `Cargo.toml`. For a machine learning project, you might want to include compiler flags that enable specific CPU or GPU features for better performance.

```
[profile.release]

opt-level = 3

lto = true
```

Packaging and Distributing the Project

Once the project is built in release mode, the compiled binaries are placed in the `target/release` directory. You can distribute these binaries directly, or package them into a compressed format like `.tar.gz` for Linux. To create a `.tar.gz` package, navigate to the `target/release` directory and run `tar -czvf simple_rust_program.tar.gz simple_rust_program`. Next, you have a compressed file containing your project's binary, which can be distributed.

Following these steps will help you prepare your basic Rust project for a proper release. If your project is well-prepared for release, it will be easy to use, perform well, and not have any dependencies that are outdated or insecure. This will allow for wider user acceptance.

Summary

This chapter covered a lot of ground in Rust programming, mostly with an eye toward getting you ready to work on machine learning projects. To get a feel for Rust syntax and key libraries like ndarray, we began by writing a rudimentary program that does array operations. Before moving on to more advanced machine learning projects, this was a significant way to get a feel for the language. We also learned the value of a clean project structure, highlighting how a logical folder layout may help with code organization and overall development efficiency.

We introduced IntelliJ Rust, a JetBrains IDE tailored for Rust development, as a way to upgrade from a text editor to a more powerful IDE. Smart code completion, robust debugging tools, and smooth integration with Cargo, Rust's package management, are just a few of the many features offered by the IDE. This environment provides a complete framework that may significantly improve coding speed and project management, making it a significant choice for constructing complex machine learning algorithms.

Another important point that we learned is the need of proper dependency management. In order to get the most out of Cargo, we investigated the best ways to manage dependencies, assign version numbers, and tailor build profiles. In order to get your project ready for release, you must follow these steps. This will guarantee that your code is efficient, user-friendly, and functional. In addition, we distributed the built binaries after going through the release process of a Rust project, which demonstrated the significance of code optimization, version control, and documentation.

The emphasis of this chapter has been on practical implementation. This book will walk you through every step of using Rust for machine learning, from configuring your development environment to organizing your project and getting it ready for release.

CHAPTER 2: DATA WRANGLING WITH RUST

Introduction

This chapter focuses on the crucial aspect of data preparation for machine learning applications. At least some computer skills and knowledge of data science are needed to do this with Rust. To begin, we will learn about data cleaning, which is an essential component of every project that is driven by data. Data cleaning encompasses the process of eliminating or rectifying abnormalities, inconsistencies, and inaccuracies present in your data. In order to accommodate the requirements of most machine learning algorithms, we will examine the process of converting categorical data into a numerical format. Furthermore, we will explore methodologies for detecting and managing outliers, which have the potential to significantly distort the outcomes of machine learning algorithms.

After completing the process of data cleaning, we will now proceed to the task of feature engineering. In this practical demonstration, we will explore techniques for enhancing the prediction capabilities of our machine learning models by transforming or generating new features based on current ones. Feature engineering encompasses a variety of operations, including standardizing and adjusting features, as well as more intricate jobs such as generating polynomial features and introducing interaction terms. This chapter will also explore Rust libraries that are suitable for various tasks, including practical, hands-on examples throughout. Feature engineering plays a crucial role in enhancing the performance of machine learning models, making it an essential step in the data preparation process.

Another crucial element we will address is the management of missing values. The issue of incomplete or sparse data is frequently encountered in machine learning, and the manner in which missing values are handled can have a substantial impact on the effectiveness of your model. We will examine various approaches such as deletion, imputation, and utilizing algorithms that possess inherent capabilities to handle missing variables. These strategies are essential for guaranteeing the utmost accuracy and completeness of the data you input into your machine learning algorithms. We will examine Rust libraries and packages that can aid with these tasks, including practical demonstrations to reinforce your comprehension.

To conclude this chapter, we will address the topics of data export, as well as the serialization and deserialization of data. After completing the process of cleaning and preprocessing your data, it may be necessary to export it into other formats to accommodate various purposes, such as sharing with other systems or conducting further analysis. Serialization is the act of transforming data structures or object states into a format that is convenient for storage and subsequent reconstruction. Deserialization is the inverse of that procedure. We will examine different file types such as CSV, JSON, and binary, and acquire the skills to manipulate them. This is essential for machine learning applications where the model and its data may require frequent saving and loading.

Upon completion of this chapter, you will possess the necessary knowledge and skills to proficiently perform data preparation, a crucial prerequisite for successful machine learning. By utilizing realistic examples and interactive demos, you will acquire the skills to effectively cleanse, manipulate, and oversee your data. This will establish a minimal groundwork for the development of our upcoming chapters' machine learning models.

This chapter focuses on the crucial aspect of data preparation for machine learning applications. At least some computer skills and knowledge of data science are needed to do this with Rust. Data cleaning encompasses the process of eliminating or rectifying abnormalities, inconsistencies, and inaccuracies present in your data. In order to accommodate the requirements of most machine learning algorithms, we will examine the process of converting categorical data into a numerical format. Furthermore, we will explore methodologies for detecting and managing outliers, which have the potential to significantly distort the outcomes of machine learning algorithms.

After completing the process of data cleaning, we will now proceed to the task of feature engineering. In this practical demonstration, we will explore techniques for enhancing the prediction capabilities of our machine learning models by transforming or generating new features based on current ones. Feature engineering encompasses a variety of operations, including standardizing and adjusting features, as well as more intricate jobs such as generating polynomial features and introducing interaction terms. This chapter will also explore Rust libraries that are suitable for various tasks, including practical, hands-on examples throughout. Feature engineering plays a crucial role in enhancing the performance of machine learning models, making it an essential step in the data preparation process.

Another crucial element we will address is the management of missing values. The issue of incomplete or sparse data is frequently encountered in machine learning, and the manner in which missing values are handled can have a substantial impact on the effectiveness of your model. We will examine various approaches such as deletion, imputation, and utilizing algorithms that possess inherent capabilities to handle missing variables. These strategies are essential for guaranteeing the utmost accuracy and completeness of the data you input into your machine learning algorithms. We will examine Rust libraries and packages that can aid with these tasks, including practical demonstrations to reinforce your comprehension.

To conclude this chapter, we will address the topics of data export, as well as the serialization and deserialization of data. After completing the process of cleaning and preprocessing your data, it may be necessary to export it into other formats to accommodate various purposes, such as sharing with other systems or conducting further analysis. Serialization is the act of transforming data structures or object states into a format that is convenient for storage and subsequent reconstruction. Deserialization is the inverse of that procedure. We will examine different file types such as CSV, JSON, and binary, and acquire the skills to manipulate them. This is essential for machine learning applications where the model and its data may require frequent saving and loading.

Upon completion of this chapter, you will possess the necessary knowledge and skills to proficiently perform data preparation, a crucial prerequisite for successful machine learning. By utilizing realistic examples and interactive demos, you will acquire the skills to effectively cleanse, manipulate, and oversee your data. This will establish a minimal groundwork for the development of our upcoming chapters' machine learning models.

Read CSV Files

At very first of this chapter, we will explore on reading CSV files, for example the heart rate prediction dataset heart_attack_prediction_dataset.csv available to download from the GitforGits github repo as below:

https://raw.githubusercontent.com/kittenpub/database-repository/main/heart_attack_prediction_dataset.csv

We will refer to this heart rate prediction dataset for all the machine learning projects and sample programs in all the upcoming chapters.

Reading CSV files is a fundamental skill in data preparation for machine learning, as CSV is a commonly used format for storing large datasets. For this, we will employ the csv crate, which is one of the most widely used libraries for handling CSV data . This library not only allows for reading and writing CSV files but also provides a range of features for dealing with headers, specific fields, and even ser/de operations.

Adding CSV Crate and File I/O Libraries

Start by including the csv crate and Rust's File I/O libraries in your Cargo.toml:

```
[dependencies]

csv = "1.1"
```

Then, in your main.rs, include the necessary imports:

```
use std::error::Error;

use std::fs::File;

use std::io::Read;

use csv::Reader;
```

Reading CSV File

Reading a CSV file involves creating a Reader object and then iterating through each record. Given below is a simple example to read the CSV file and print each record:

```
fn main() -> Result<(), Box<dyn Error>> {
```

```
let mut file = File::open("path/to/heart_attack_prediction_dataset.csv")?;

let mut reader = Reader::from_reader(file);


for result in reader.records() {

let record = result?;

println!("{:?}", record);

}


Ok(())

}
```

Replace "path/to/heart_attack_prediction_dataset.csv" with the actual path to your downloaded CSV file. This code will print each record in the CSV file. The Reader object takes care of parsing the CSV format, and we simply iterate through each record using reader.records().

Dealing with Headers and Specific Fields

If your CSV file contains headers, you can skip them using reader.headers()?.clone();. Additionally, if we are only interested in specific fields, you can directly access them using the header's name or the field's index. For example:

```
let headers = reader.headers()?.clone();

println!("Headers: {:?}", headers);


for result in reader.records() {

let record = result?;
```

```
let heart_rate: u32 = record["heart_rate"].parse()?;

println!("Heart Rate: {}", heart_rate);

}
```

This will print only the "heart_rate" field from each record, assuming that "heart_rate" is one of the headers in your CSV file.

Data Validation

When reading data, especially for machine learning purposes, validation is crucial. The `csv` crate returns a `Result` type for each record, allowing you to handle errors gracefully. This is vital when dealing with large datasets where some records may be malformed or missing crucial data. The use of Rust's `Result` type ensures that you can catch these issues at the time of data reading, making your data preparation phase robust and reliable.

Storing Records in a Data Structure

Often, you will want to store the read records in some data structure for further manipulation or analysis. Rust's strong type system allows you to define a struct that matches the schema of your CSV file, making it easier to manipulate the data later.

For example:

```
#[derive(Debug, Deserialize)]

struct Record {

 age: u32,

 gender: String,

 heart_rate: u32,

 // add other fields

}

let mut reader = Reader::from_reader(file);

let mut records: Vec<Record> = Vec::new();
```

```
for result in reader.deserialize() {
 let record: Record = result?;
 records.push(record);
}
```

In the above program, we defined a Record struct that will hold individual records from the CSV file. We then store each Record in a vector named records.

You now know how to handle headers and certain fields in a CSV file, read it, and store the entries in a custom data structure. These processes are essential for prepping data, which is a key step in creating machine learning models.

Data Cleaning with Polars

When getting data ready for machine learning, data cleaning is a must. We got a dataset for heart rate prediction; now what? Well, we now pretend that it has some usual problems, such noisy data, outliers, or missing values. Rust offers several libraries for data cleaning or manipulation, and one of the prominent ones is polars. This library is highly performant and offers a multitude of functions for efficient data manipulation, which is especially useful for large datasets commonly found in machine learning projects.

Installing Polars and Importing Data

To use polars, add it to your Cargo.toml under the [dependencies] section:

```
polars = "0.14"
```

Once the dependency is added, you can read the CSV file into a DataFrame. DataFrames are two-dimensional size-mutable and potentially heterogeneous tabular data structures with labeled axes (rows and columns).

Following is how you can read a CSV file into a DataFrame:

```
extern crate polars;

use polars::prelude::*;

fn main() -> Result<()> {
```

```
let file = File::open("path/to/heart_attack_prediction_dataset.csv")?;
let df = CsvReader::new(file)
.infer_schema(Some(100))
.has_header(true)
.finish()?;
}
```

Handling Missing Values

One major problem with machine learning datasets is missing values. polars provides several methods to handle missing values, such as filling them with a specific value (fill_none) or using forward or backward filling methods (fill_none_forward or fill_none_backward).

For example, to fill missing values in a column named "heart_rate" with the mean:

```
let mean_heart_rate = df.column("heart_rate")?.mean()?;
let new_df = df.with_column(
 df.column("heart_rate")?
 .fillna(mean_heart_rate)?
);
```

Removing Outliers

The effectiveness of ML models can be drastically impacted by outliers. If you filter the rows according to a certain condition, you can get rid of them.

For example, you can exclude extreme values, such as heart rates below 40 or above 200, if you know they don't represent reality:

```
let filtered_df = df.filter(
 (col("heart_rate").gt(40)) & (col("heart_rate").lt(200))
```

```
)?;
```

Normalizing and Scaling Features

It's often beneficial to normalize or scale your features, especially when they have different ranges. polars doesn't have built-in functions for normalization, but you can easily do this using basic DataFrame operations.

For example, to normalize the "heart_rate" column:

```
let max = df.column("heart_rate")?.max()?;

let min = df.column("heart_rate")?.min()?;

let normalized_df = df.with_column(

 (col("heart_rate") - min) / (max - min)

);
```

Data Transformation

Sometimes, the raw features may not provide enough information, and you may need to create new features from existing ones. This is known as feature engineering, and polars DataFrame operations can be really useful here.

For example, if you want to create a new feature that is the square of the heart rate:

```
let transformed_df = df.with_column(

 col("heart_rate").pow(2)

);
```

You may clean and prepare your dataset for machine learning more efficiently by using polars and its extensive collection of DataFrame methods. The performance-oriented design of the library makes it ideal for handling massive datasets, providing a practical means of performing data manipulations commonly needed in machine learning initiatives.

Feature Engineering

An essential part of getting your dataset ready for ML is feature engineering. Making new features from old ones or changing features to make them better fits is what it is all about. The ability of machine learning algorithms to make predictions can be significantly improved with well designed features. Since we are already working and are now familiar with the polars library, you have the right set of tools at your use to perform various feature engineering tasks quite effectively.

Creating Polynomial Features

Polynomial features are those features created by raising an existing feature to a power. For example, if you have a feature "heart_rate," you can create a new feature "heart_rate_squared" by squaring each value in the "heart_rate" column. Following is how to create polynomial features for the "heart_rate" column:

```
let df_poly = df.with_column(

 col("heart_rate").pow(2).alias("heart_rate_squared")

);
```

One question might come to your mind is, why might this be useful? Polynomial features can capture the effect of the magnitude of a feature more than the feature itself. This can be especially beneficial for regression algorithms or algorithms that make mathematical assumptions about the linearity between features and the output variable.

Creating Interaction Terms

Interaction terms consider the effect of two features combined. For example, if your dataset has features like "age" and "cholesterol_level," an interaction term would be "age" multiplied by "cholesterol_level." In mathematical models, individual features may not have a significant impact, but their interaction might. Following is how to create an interaction term:

```
let df_interact = df.with_column(

 (col("age") * col("cholesterol_level")).alias("age_cholesterol_interaction")

);
```

Categorical Variable Encoding

Machine learning algorithms generally work with numerical input. So, if your dataset includes categorical variables, you will need to encode them into numbers. One common technique is one-hot encoding, which converts each unique category value into a new categorical feature and assigns a binary value of 1 or 0. While polars doesn't have built-in one-hot encoding, you can create such columns manually using conditional statements:

```
let df_encoded = df.with_column(

 when(col("gender").eq("Male"))

 .then(1)

 .otherwise(0)

 .alias("is_male")

);
```

Binning and Discretization

Sometimes numerical features are converted into categorical features, known as 'binning' or 'discretization.' For example, you might want to convert a continuous feature like "age" into age groups. This can be useful in scenarios where the exact age might not be as relevant as the age group.

```
let df_binned = df.with_column(

 when(col("age").lt(30))

 .then("Young")

 .when(col("age").lt(60))

 .then("Middle-aged")

 .otherwise("Old")

 .alias("age_group")

);
```

Normalization and Standardization

Though we covered this in the previous 'data cleaning' section, it is also a form of feature engineering. Normalizing scales all numeric variables to a standard range, usually [0,1], while standardization transforms data to have a mean of zero and a standard deviation of 1. These techniques can be vital for distance-based algorithms like k-NN or gradient descent-based algorithms like neural networks.

```
// Normalization

let max = df.column("heart_rate")?.max()?;

let min = df.column("heart_rate")?.min()?;

let df_normalized = df.with_column(

 ((col("heart_rate") - lit(min)) / (lit(max) - lit(min))).alias("normalized_heart_rate")

);


// Standardization

let mean = df.column("heart_rate")?.mean()?;

let std_dev = df.column("heart_rate")?.std()?;

let df_standardized = df.with_column(

 ((col("heart_rate") - lit(mean)) / lit(std_dev)).alias("standardized_heart_rate")

);
```

Feature engineering offers a means to improve the quality of your dataset, hence enhancing the accuracy and effectiveness of your machine learning models. The goal of each strategy varies, and the problem we are attempting to address will determine the techniques you choose.

Plotters and Data Visualization

Data visualization is a crucial aspect of any data analysis or machine learning workflow. It allows you to understand the distribution, tendencies, and outliers in your dataset. For Rust, one of the prominent libraries for creating plots is `plotters`. It is a highly flexible and customizable plotting library that can output a variety of plot types.

Install Plotters

First, add the **plotters** crate to your **Cargo.toml**:

```
[dependencies]

plotters = "0.3"
```

This will download and compile the **plotters** library, making it available for use in your Rust program.

Basic Plot Creation

To create a basic scatter plot of, say, "age" against "heart_rate," you can start by setting up a drawing area and specifying the ranges for the x and y-axes. The drawing area will host your plot, and it is where all the elements like axes, labels, and points will be drawn.

```
use plotters::prelude::*;

let root = BitMapBackend::new("path/to/output.png", (640, 480)).into_drawing_area();

root.fill(&WHITE)?;

let mut chart = ChartBuilder::on(&root)

 .caption("Age vs. Heart Rate", ("Arial", 40).into_font())

 .margin(5)

 .x_label_area_size(30)

 .y_label_area_size(30)

 .build_cartesian_2d(0u32..100u32, 0u32..200u32)?;

chart.configure_mesh().draw()?;
```

Populating Data Points

Now that the drawing area and axes are set up, you can populate it with data points. Assuming you have a DataFrame **df** from **polars** containing the columns "age" and "heart_rate," you can iterate through these columns to plot each point.

```
let age_series = df.column("age")?.to_array()?;

let heart_rate_series = df.column("heart_rate")?.to_array()?;

for (age, heart_rate) in age_series.iter().zip(heart_rate_series.iter()) {

 chart.draw_series(PointSeries::of_element(

 [*age as u32, *heart_rate as u32],

 5,

 &RED,

 &|c, s, st| {

 return EmptyElement::at(c) + Circle::new((0, 0), *s, st.filled());

 },

 ))?;

}
```

This will plot each (age, heart_rate) pair as a red point on the chart.

Advanced Customization

plotters offers a multitude of customization options. For example, you can add labels to the x and y-axes to make the plot more informative.

```
chart

 .configure_mesh()

 .x_desc("Age")

 .y_desc("Heart Rate")
```

```
.draw()?;
```

Additionally, you can also configure the grid, tick marks, and other graphical elements to make your plot more readable and aesthetically pleasing. The library supports various types of plots like line plots, bar charts, and histograms, providing options to suit various data visualization needs.

Plotting Multiple Series

Often, you may want to plot multiple series on the same chart, perhaps to compare them. plotters make this straightforward. You can simply draw multiple series on the same chart instance. For example, if you have another column in your DataFrame, say "cholesterol_level," and you want to plot it alongside "heart_rate," you can do:

```
let cholesterol_series = df.column("cholesterol_level")?.to_array()?;

for cholesterol in cholesterol_series.iter() {

 chart.draw_series(PointSeries::of_element(

 [*age as u32, *cholesterol as u32],

 5,

 &BLUE,

 &|c, s, st| {

 return EmptyElement::at(c) + Circle::new((0, 0), *s, st.filled());

 },

 ))?;

}
```

This will add a new series of blue points representing "cholesterol_level" against "age."

A well-designed plot can highlight trends, patterns, and insights that are not obvious from raw data alone. The plotters library provides an efficient and adaptable approach to produce a wide range of plots, from simple scatter plots to more complex multi-series and 3D charts. Its extensive set of features and customization possibilities make it an effective tool for data visualization in the Rust community.

Data Export: JSON, Parquet, Feather and Binary

While CSV is a popular and widely accepted format, there are various more formats you may encounter or need for special purposes. These include JSON for web-based apps, Parquet and Feather for big data analytics, and native binary formats for high-performance applications. Being able to convert your data into one of these forms can be a useful ability, as each of these formats has its own set of benefits and uses.

JSON (JavaScript Object Notation)

JSON is a text-based format that is easy to read and write. It's often used in web applications and APIs. JSON files are more human-readable than CSV and allow for a hierarchical, nested data structure. However, they are not as space-efficient as CSV or binary formats, which could be a limitation for very large datasets. When you need to share data with a web service or consume data from one, we are likely to use JSON.

```
use polars::prelude::*;

use std::fs::File;

use std::io::Write;

let json_string = df.write_json();

let mut file = File::create("heart_attack_data.json")?;

file.write_all(json_string.as_bytes())?;
```

Parquet

Parquet is a columnar storage file format optimized for use with big data processing frameworks. It's highly efficient, both in terms of disk I/O and storage space, and it allows for advanced optimization techniques such as data partitioning and predicate pushdown. If we are planning to use cloud-based big data analytics services, Parquet is often the recommended file format.

```
df.write_parquet("path/to/heart_attack_data.parquet", None)?;
```

Feather

Feather is another columnar storage format, but unlike Parquet, it is optimized for speed and flexibility. It's designed to be fast whether we are reading from disk or writing to disk. If you need to interchange data between languages like Python, R, and Rust, Feather can be an excellent choice because of its language-agnostic design.

```
df.write_feather("path/to/heart_attack_data.feather")?;
```

Native Binary

For performance-critical applications, you might want to use a binary file format. Binary formats are not human-readable, but they are extremely efficient in both read and write operations. They are particularly useful when you need to save and load your data multiple times during your project, as in the case of machine learning where iterative development is common.

```
let buffer: Vec<u8> = df.write_ipc()?;

let mut file = File::create("heart_attack_data.ipc")?;

file.write_all(&buffer)?;
```

Finally, the format in which you should export your data is determined by what you need. JSON is ideal for online apps and APIs, while Parquet and Feather are ideal for large data analytics. Binary formats are better for performance-critical applications. Polars, with its various read and write methods, makes it simple to export data to these diverse formats.

Data Serialization and Deserialization

Serialization is the process of transforming a data structure or object state into a format that can be readily saved and reassembled. Deserialization is the reverse process of converting serialized data back into a fully functional data structure or object. These actions are critical in a variety of circumstances, such as data storage, network transmission, and interprocess communication. Serialization is frequently used in machine learning to save the state of trained models, whereas deserialization is used to load a previously trained model for prediction or additional training.

Understanding Serialization

A prime example of why serialization is necessary is... Assume you have trained a machine learning model. When stored in memory, this model is a complicated object with many characteristics, methods, and internal states. To utilize this model later or to deploy it in a different environment, you must save this complicated object in a form that allows it to be fully recovered. Serialization aids in transforming this complex object into a byte stream or other format that can then be saved to disk or transmitted over a network. When you want to utilize this model again, you use deserialization to turn the saved format back into the complex object, restoring its original state and functionality.

Using Serde for Serialization

Rust offers a powerful serialization and deserialization framework called Serde, which stands for SERialize/DEserialize. It's both performant and provides mechanisms for custom serialization logic. To use Serde, you first need to include it in your Cargo.toml:

```
[dependencies]

serde = { version = "1.0", features = ["derive"] }

serde_json = "1.0"
```

Once you have Serde and its JSON support (you can also use other formats), you can serialize almost any data structure . For example, if you have a DataFrame named df, you can serialize it into a JSON string as follows:

```
extern crate serde_json;

use serde::Serialize;

#[derive(Serialize)]

struct Record {

 age: u32,

 heart_rate: u32,

 // ... other fields

}

let records: Vec<Record> = df_to_records(df); // Assume df_to_records converts a DataFrame to Vec<Record>

let serialized_data = serde_json::to_string(&records)?;
```

Deserialization in Rust

Deserialization is the reverse process. We assume you have a JSON string that you want to convert back into a DataFrame. You can do this by defining a struct that matches the JSON structure and then using Serde to populate this struct:

```
use serde::Deserialize;

#[derive(Deserialize)]

struct Record {

 age: u32,

 heart_rate: u32,

 // ... other fields

}

let deserialized_data: Vec<Record> = serde_json::from_str(&serialized_data)?;

let df = records_to_df(deserialized_data); // Assume records_to_df converts Vec<Record> back to a DataFrame
```

Custom Serialization and Deserialization

Sometimes the default serialization and deserialization behavior may not be suitable for your specific needs. Serde allows for custom serialization and deserialization through attributes and custom functions. For example, if you want to serialize only those records where the age is above 30, you can write custom functions and annotate your struct accordingly.

Both, serialization and deserialization are fundamental techniques that enable you to store and restore complex data structures, making them particularly useful in machine learning applications for saving models and datasets. Rust's Serde library provides a comprehensive, efficient, and flexible means to perform these operations.

Summary

During this chapter, we undertook an extensive exploration of data preparation and administration, which are fundamental components of any machine learning endeavor. We started by cleaning the data using Rust's polars library to deal with outliers, missing values, and feature normalization, as well as other important issues. To lay the groundwork for high-quality data analysis, examples showed how to alter a DataFrame to prepare it for machine learning techniques.

What followed was an investigation into feature engineering, where we learned to construct polynomial features, interaction terms, and other related concepts. As a result, the dataset gets improved and becomes more useful for ML models. Binding, normalization, and classification are just a few of the shared approaches that enrich raw data with more information, making it more useful for advanced algorithms.

We then proceeded to dive into data visualization with the plotters. In addition to being visually appealing, data visualization is essential for gaining insight into the trends and patterns included within the data. We covered the fundamentals of creating a plot, adding data points to it, and modifying it to make it easier to read and understand.

Lastly, we compared and contrasted several data storage and transmission formats, such as JSON, Parquet, and Feather, to learn about their benefits and the situations in which they excel. Data serialization and deserialization, which we discussed briefly, are fundamental ideas that allow us to store and retrieve complicated data structures, such as machine learning models. The Serde library helped us comprehend these procedures in practice, which solidified our knowledge of the complete data lifecycle in ML projects.

CHAPTER 3: LINEAR REGRESSION BY EXAMPLE

Introduction to Linear Regression

Overview

Linear regression is among the most widely used statistical models in machine learning and data science. At its core, linear regression aims to model the relationship between a dependent variable and one or more independent variables by fitting a linear equation to the observed data. The model's simplicity and interpretability make it a staple in fields as varied as economics, biology, engineering, and, of course, machine learning. Even though it may seem elementary, the model's straightforwardness is its strength, offering a clear, interpretable way to represent complex relationships in a digestible form.

One of the most innovative aspects of linear regression is its ability to make predictions. In machine learning, the primary goal is often to build a model that can generalize well to new, unseen data. Linear regression's predictive power is astonishingly robust for such a simple model. The reason it works so well in prediction scenarios lies in its mathematical foundation. By minimizing the sum of squared differences between the observed values and the values predicted by the model, linear regression arrives at the "line of best fit." This line serves as a simplified representation of the complex relationships between variables, which can then be used to make predictions about new data points.

Linear regression also provides deep insights into the relationships between variables. The coefficients in the linear equation represent the extent and direction of the impact that each independent variable has on the dependent variable. For instance, in a healthcare context, a linear regression model could show how different factors like age, cholesterol levels, and exercise affect the risk of heart disease. The coefficients could indicate the extent to which each of these factors increases or decreases the risk, providing actionable insights for both healthcare providers and patients.

While the basic linear regression model is simple, it serves as the foundation for more complex models and techniques. For instance, logistic regression, used for classification problems, is an extension of linear regression. Further, techniques like ridge and lasso regression extend linear models to handle collinearity between variables and prevent overfitting. There's also polynomial regression, which, despite its name, is a type of linear regression that can model curvilinear relationships by adding polynomial terms to the equation.

Linear regression has been widely adopted in various industries for practical applications. For example, in finance, it is used for risk assessment; in healthcare, for predicting patient outcomes; and in sales, for forecasting future revenues. With Rust's growing ecosystem of machine learning libraries, implementing linear regression models has become more efficient and reliable. Libraries like `linregress` offer simple APIs to fit, predict, and evaluate linear models, taking advantage of Rust's performance and type safety. As we proceed to implement linear regression models, we will see firsthand how this seemingly simple technique can provide a wealth of information and utility.

Linear Regression: Problem Statement

Definition

The problem statement for using linear regression on the dataset of heart attack predictions needs to be defined. The basic goal is to predict a quantitative measure, say "heart rate," using other relevant independent factors such as age, cholesterol level, and blood pressure. The goal of using this regression will be "to develop a linear regression model that can predict a patient's heart rate based on variables such as age, cholesterol level, and blood pressure." Because we want to predict a continuous outcome variable ("Heart Rate") using one or more predictor variables, this problem description fits nicely with the linear regression model.

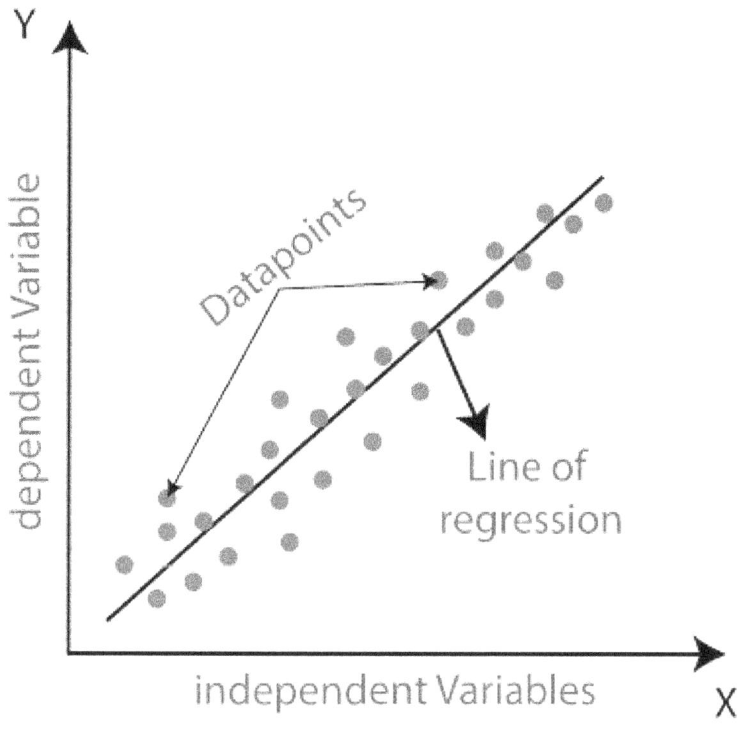

Fig 3.1 Linear Regression

Variable Selection and Feature Engineering

Since the dataset includes multiple variables, the first step is to select which ones are most relevant for predicting heart rate. While the previous chapter covered generic feature engineering techniques, this is more about domain-specific feature selection. Medical literature could help in identifying variables that have been shown to impact heart rate. Variables like age, cholesterol level, and blood pressure might be good starting points. Once selected, you can create a new DataFrame containing only these columns.

```
let selected_columns = ["age", "cholesterol_level", "blood_pressure"];

let df_selected = df.select(selected_columns);
```

Data Splitting

It is typical practice in machine learning to divide a dataset into two parts: training and testing sets. The training set trains the model, while the testing set evaluates its performance. We can go on to this stage now that the data has been cleaned. We could use 70% of the data for training and the other 30% for testing.

```
let (train_df, test_df) = df_selected.rand_split(0.7);
```

Feature Scaling

While basic preprocessing has been learned, it is critical to learn feature scaling, specifically for linear regression. Different variables may be in different units, and a wide range of values for one variable can dominate the others in the model. This issue can be addressed by standardizing or normalizing the features. We can normalize the features to have a mean of zero and a standard deviation of one. We may go into ridge and lasso regression later on, but feature scaling is crucial for these methods.

```
let train_df = train_df.standardize(Some(selected_columns));

let test_df = test_df.standardize(Some(selected_columns));
```

Target Variable

Finally, we now isolate the target variable, which is "Heart Rate" in our case. Separating the dependent and independent variables will make it easier to feed the data into our linear regression model.

```
let train_x = train_df.drop("Heart Rate");

let train_y = train_df.column("Heart Rate");
```

```
let test_x = test_df.drop("Heart Rate");

let test_y = test_df.column("Heart Rate");
```

We are now ready to perform linear regression after defining the problem statement and preparing the data. The predictor variables are age, cholesterol, and blood pressure, while the target variable is heart rate. We've also separated the data into training and testing sets and scaled the features to ensure they all contribute equally to the model. In the following section, we will look at how to design the linear regression model, train it on the data, and evaluate its performance.

Popular Linear Regression Strategies

Before we move on, we take a look at the methods that are typically utilized when performing linear regression. These approaches or procedures provide a structured road for model building, guaranteeing that the process is systematic and produces repeatable outcomes.

Exploratory Data Analysis (EDA)

Even if you've cleaned and selected variables for your dataset, you should run an EDA before getting into modeling. This process assists you in understanding the data distribution, identifying patterns, and detecting anomalies. Visualizations such as scatter plots for continuous variables and box plots for categorical variables are quite useful. EDA enables you to make informed decisions regarding feature selection and model parameters. For example, if two features are highly correlated, combining them may result in multicollinearity, which can have an impact on model performance.

Hypothesis Testing

It is essential to formulate hypotheses regarding the expected relationships between variables before using linear regression. One could, for example, hypothesize that "increased age will lead to a higher heart rate." The model then either validates or invalidates these ideas. It's an important phase since it helps determine whether the model's results make logical and empirical sense.

Model Selection

There are various types of linear regression, including basic linear regression, multiple linear regression, and polynomial regression. The decision is determined by the number of predictor variables and the nature of the relationship (linear or nonlinear) between the dependent and independent variables. If you have numerous predictor variables and feel that the relationship is not strictly linear, you may want to use polynomial regression.

Feature Interaction Terms

Sometimes the impact of two or more variables on the dependent variable is interactive rather than additive. In such circumstances, interaction terms may be introduced. For example, the combined effect of age and cholesterol level on heart rate may differ from the separate effects. Adding interaction terms can help capture these complicated relationships, but it should be done with caution to prevent overfitting.

Model Training and Validation

Once the model type and features have been determined, the following step is to train the model. This entails passing the training data into an algorithm to determine the coefficients. After training, the model must be validated to ensure that it applies well to new data. This is where the testing setup comes into play. Metrics such as Root Mean Square Error (RMSE) and R-squared can be utilized for this purpose.

Iterative Refinement

Machine learning is a process that is iterative. Based on the insights discovered during training and validation, it may be necessary to get back to feature selection, engineering, or even EDA. Perhaps a characteristic you overlooked initially proves to be crucial, or perhaps the model is overfitting and requires regularization.

Interpreting Results and Making Decisions

The next, and sometimes forgotten, step is to interpret the model's conclusions in the context of the problem we are trying to address. The coefficients indicate the magnitude and direction of the effect that each independent variable has on the dependent variable. These should be read carefully before making data-driven decisions.

By following this organized strategy, you can ensure that the linear regression model you create is both robust and interpretable, making it a dependable tool for prediction and decision-making. Now that we've established a consistent methodology, the next step would be to apply linear regression to our dataset.

Implement Linear Regression Model

To implement a linear regression model, we can use the `linregress` library. It's a simple but powerful library for linear regression, which can handle both single-variable (simple) and multi-variable (multiple) linear regression.

Firstly, we now add the `linregress` package to our `Cargo.toml`:

```
[dependencies]

linregress = "0.4"
```

Model Training

We start by training the model. Given that we've already prepared our data and split it into training and testing sets, we can proceed to fit the model. Below is a code snippet to perform this operation:

```
extern crate linregress;

use linregress::RegressionModel;

let model = RegressionModel::least_squares(&train_x, &train_y).unwrap();
```

We use the least squares method to fit the model. The function takes in the training set features (train_x) and the labels (train_y) and returns a fitted model.

Interpreting Coefficients

After fitting, the model object contains the coefficients (also known as weights or parameters) for each feature. These coefficients tell us the impact of each feature on the target variable, which in our case is heart rate.

```
let coefficients = model.parameters;
```

Suppose the coefficients for age, cholesterol level, and blood pressure are 0.3, 0.2, and 0.5, respectively. This means that a one-unit increase in age would result in a 0.3-unit increase in heart rate, holding all else constant. Similarly, a one-unit increase in cholesterol level and blood pressure would result in a 0.2 and 0.5 increase in heart rate, respectively.

Model Prediction and Validation

Once we've trained the model, the next step is to use it for prediction and then validate its performance. We can use our test set for this purpose.

```
let predictions = model.predict(&test_x).unwrap();
```

To validate the model, we can use metrics like Root Mean Square Error (RMSE) or R-squared, which give us an idea of how well the model performs.

```
let rmse = ((&test_y - &predictions).powi(2)).mean().sqrt();
```

An RMSE value closer to 0 indicates a better fit, while a high value suggests that the model may not be fitting the data well.

Iterative Refinement

Based on the RMSE or other metrics, you might need to go back and refine the model. Maybe you will include more features, add interaction terms, or even try a different kind of regression (like ridge or lasso for regularization).

Overall, we used the linregress library to train a linear regression model, then we used the coefficients to determine the importance of features, and finally, we used RMSE to validate the model. This hands-on approach teaches you not only theoretical understanding but also practical skills for applying linear regression to real-world problems.

Other Linear Regression Libraries

While linregress provides a straightforward way to implement linear regression models, there are other libraries that offer more features, flexibility, and customization options. Knowing these alternative libraries can be quite advantageous, as different projects may have different requirements, some of which may not be fully met by a single package.

Rustlearn

Rustlearn is another machine learning library for Rust that includes an array of algorithms, linear regression being one of them. What sets Rustlearn apart is its focus on compatibility with other Rust libraries. This allows for easier integration and a more unified workflow. The library also aims for ease of use, offering a simple API for both training and prediction. You can include it in your project by adding the following to your Cargo.toml:

```
[dependencies]

rustlearn = "0.5"
```

In Rustlearn, model fitting and prediction are very straightforward:

```
use rustlearn::prelude::*;
```

```
use rustlearn::linear_models::sgdclassifier::Hyperparameters;

let mut model = Hyperparameters::new(3).build();

model.fit(&train_x, &train_y).unwrap();
```

The benefit of **Rustlearn** is its focus on a more generalized machine learning workflow. While **linregress** is specialized for linear regression, **Rustlearn** provides a more comprehensive ecosystem, which can be beneficial for projects that require multiple types of models.

Smartcore

Smartcore is a versatile machine learning library that aims to bring the power of scikit-learn to the Rust ecosystem. It provides a range of machine learning algorithms, including linear regression. It's particularly useful when we are looking for a library that can handle both supervised and unsupervised learning tasks. To add it to your project, include this in your **Cargo.toml**:

```
[dependencies]

smartcore = "0.2"
```

Smartcore provides more options for data validation and preprocessing, making it a good choice for projects that require extensive data manipulation before model training:

```
use smartcore::linalg::naive::dense_matrix::DenseMatrix;

use smartcore::linear::linear_regression::LinearRegression;

let x = DenseMatrix::from_2d_array(&train_x);

let y = train_y;

let lr = LinearRegression::fit(&x, &y, Default::default()).unwrap();
```

Alumina

While not primarily a machine learning library, **Alumina** is a neural network library that also provides a range of generalized linear models, including linear regression. It's particularly beneficial when your project includes both traditional machine learning models and neural networks. It also provides a lot of options for optimization, including various gradient descent methods. To use it, you would add the following to your Cargo.toml:

```
[dependencies]

alumina = "0.3"
```

The advantage of Alumina lies in its optimization capabilities. You can tune various parameters and use different optimization techniques, making it a flexible choice for more complex projects:

```
use alumina_core::graph::Node;

use alumina_core::graph_ops::apply;

use alumina_linear::ops::linear::linear;

let input = Node::new(&[batch_size, input_size]);

let target = Node::new(&[batch_size, output_size]);

let linear_node = linear(input, target);
```

Each of these libraries brings its own set of advantages and features to the table. Rustlearn provides a simple, unified workflow, Smartcore offers extensive data manipulation and validation features, and Alumina provides advanced optimization capabilities.

Evaluate Linear Regression Performance

Evaluating the performance of a linear regression model is a critical step in the machine learning pipeline. It's not enough to simply train the model; you need to know how well it is performing on unseen data. Multiple metrics can be used for this evaluation, each offering a different perspective on the model's effectiveness. In the context of the heart rate prediction model we built using the heart attack dataset, we now explore some of these evaluation metrics.

Root Mean Square Error (RMSE)

RMSE is one of the most commonly used metrics for evaluating linear regression models. It measures the average magnitude of the errors between predicted and observed values in the dataset. A lower RMSE value indicates a better fit of the model to the data. You could calculate RMSE as follows:

```
let squared_errors = predictions.iter()
 .zip(test_y.iter())
 .map(|(pred, actual)| (pred - actual).powi(2))
 .collect::<Vec<f64>>();
let rmse = (squared_errors.iter().sum::<f64>() / squared_errors.len() as f64).sqrt();
```

RMSE is sensitive to outliers, which means that a few large errors can significantly inflate the value. Therefore, it is crucial to ensure that your data doesn't contain extreme values that could skew this metric. It's also essential to remember that RMSE alone can't provide a full picture of model performance, especially if we are dealing with imbalanced or non-normal data distribution.

Coefficient of Determination (R-squared)

R-squared is another key metric used for evaluating linear models. It represents the proportion of the variance in the dependent variable that is predictable from the independent variables. It ranges from 0 to 1, where higher values indicate that the model explains a larger proportion of the variance.

```
let ss_total = test_y.iter().map(|&y| (y - test_y.mean()).powi(2)).sum::<f64>();
let ss_residual = squared_errors.iter().sum::<f64>();
let r_squared = 1.0 - (ss_residual / ss_total);
```

R-squared is beneficial because it provides a measure of how well the model's predictions match the actual data. However, it is worth noting that a high R-squared doesn't always mean the model is good. An overly complex model can 'overfit' the data, resulting in a high R-squared value but poor predictive performance.

Mean Absolute Error (MAE)

While RMSE gives a sense of the magnitude of the error, Mean Absolute Error (MAE) provides a clearer picture of the average error in the predictions. MAE is less sensitive to outliers compared to RMSE, making it a more robust metric in certain scenarios.

```
let mae = predictions.iter()
```

```
.zip(test_y.iter())

.map(|(pred, actual)| (pred - actual).abs())

.sum::<f64>() / test_y.len() as f64;
```

MAE is easy to understand and explain, making it a good choice when you need to justify the model's performance to stakeholders who may not be familiar with machine learning terminology.

Residual Plots

While numerical metrics provide a quantitative evaluation, residual plots offer a qualitative view. A residual plot shows the difference between the observed and predicted values for each data point. Ideally, these residuals should be randomly scattered around zero.

```
let residuals = predictions.iter()

.zip(test_y.iter())

.map(|(pred, actual)| pred - actual)

.collect::<Vec<f64>>();
```

Plotting these residuals against the predicted values can reveal patterns that might not be apparent through numerical metrics alone. For instance, if the residuals show a clear trend, it might suggest that the model is not capturing some underlying pattern in the data.

Each of these above metrics should be used in conjunction to get an accurate assessment, enabling you to fine-tune the model for better results.

Save and Reload Model

Once you've trained a model, you typically want to save its state so that you can either share it with others or simply reload it later to make predictions on new data. There are multiple ways to serialize and deserialize machine learning models, depending on how you plan to use them.

Serialization using Serde

The Serde library is one of the most commonly used serialization libraries . It provides a framework for serializing and deserializing Rust data structures efficiently and generically. To use Serde for saving and loading your model, first include it in your Cargo.toml:

```
[dependencies]

serde = "1.0"

serde_derive = "1.0"

serde_json = "1.0"
```

After including the Serde library, you can serialize your model into a JSON format. Given below is a simple example:

```
extern crate serde_json;

use serde::Serialize;

use serde::Deserialize;

#[derive(Serialize, Deserialize)]

struct LinearModel {

 coefficients: Vec<f64>,

 intercept: f64,

}

let model = LinearModel {

 coefficients: vec![0.3, 0.2, 0.5],

 intercept: 1.0,

};

let serialized_model = serde_json::to_string(&model).unwrap();
```

In the above program, the LinearModel struct represents a simplified linear regression model with coefficients and an intercept. We then serialize this struct into a JSON string.

Writing and Reading Files

Once the model is serialized into a JSON string, the next step is to write this string into a file. Rust's standard library provides a straightforward way to read and write files.

```
use std::fs::File;

use std::io::prelude::*;



// Writing to a file

let mut file = File::create("linear_model.json").unwrap();

file.write_all(serialized_model.as_bytes()).unwrap();



// Reading from a file

let mut file = File::open("linear_model.json").unwrap();

let mut contents = String::new();

file.read_to_string(&mut contents).unwrap();
```

In this code snippet, we first create a new file called `linear_model.json` and write the serialized JSON string into it. Later, we read this file back into a string.

Deserialization and Model Loading

After reading the serialized model from the file, you can deserialize it back into a Rust struct using Serde.

```
let deserialized_model: LinearModel = serde_json::from_str(&contents).unwrap();
```

This will convert the JSON string back into a `LinearModel` struct, effectively reloading your model. You can then use this deserialized model to make new predictions.

```
let new_prediction = deserialized_model.coefficients.iter().zip(new_data.iter())
```

```
.map(|(c, x)| c * x)

.sum::<f64>() + deserialized_model.intercept;
```

In this snippet, new_data is a vector containing the features for a new observation. We use the deserialized model's coefficients and intercept to make a prediction.

The above methods work well for simpler models like linear regression. However, as you move towards more complex models like neural networks, the serialization and deserialization process can get complicated due to the network's architecture, learned parameters, and other hyperparameters. You might need to serialize each component separately and use custom serialization and deserialization methods to ensure that the model can be accurately recreated.

Linear Regression Model Deployment

The deployment procedure varies widely depending on your project's individual requirements, however there are common ways that can be used as a blueprint for deploying linear regression models, or any other machine learning model, in a Rust-based environment.

The first step in deploying a machine learning model is to decide how it will be used. There are a few common tactics. One approach is to embed the model directly into a server-side Rust application. Another option is to embed the model in a web service, which might be constructed with frameworks such as Rocket or Actix and accessed by HTTP queries. The chosen strategy will govern the remaining deployment processes, including the technology used and the infrastructure required.

Packaging the Model

Regardless of the chosen deployment strategy, the model must be packaged along with any dependencies. As we've serialized the model into a JSON file, this file should be included in the deployment package. For Rust, the package can be built using Cargo, which will compile your code and package it with all the required dependencies.

```
cargo build --release
```

This command builds your project in release mode, placing the compiled binary in the target/release directory. This binary includes the logic for loading the model and making predictions, and it can be distributed and executed on other systems that have the appropriate runtime environment.

Creating a Web Service

If you chose to deploy your model as a web service, the next step would be to wrap your model in an HTTP server. Frameworks like Rocket and Actix provide the tools needed to build robust, high-performance web services. Given below is a simplified Rocket example that loads a linear regression model and uses it to make a prediction based on JSON input:

```
#[post("/", data = "<input_data>")]

fn make_prediction(input_data: Json<InputData>) -> Json<OutputData> {

 let model = load_model("model.json"); // Function to load your model

 let prediction = model.predict(input_data);

 Json(OutputData { prediction })

}
```

In this code snippet, the make_prediction function is an HTTP POST endpoint that takes some input_data, makes a prediction using the loaded model, and returns the prediction.

Deploying to Server

Once your model and application are packaged, the next step is to move this package to a server where it will be run. If your application is a simple binary, this process is as straightforward as copying the binary to the server and executing it. If you've created a web service, you will also need to ensure that your server is equipped to handle HTTP requests, which may involve setting up a reverse proxy with software like Nginx or Apache.

Monitoring and Logging

After deployment, it is crucial to set up monitoring and logging to ensure that the model is performing as expected. This is not just about monitoring the machine's CPU and memory usage but also about keeping an eye on the model's performance metrics. You can use logging libraries like env_logger or slog to log prediction errors, latency, and other custom metrics. These logs can be shipped to a centralized logging system like Elasticsearch or Splunk for further analysis and visualization.

Versioning and Rollback

Finally, a robust deployment strategy also considers the need for version control and rollback options. This involves keeping track of which model version is deployed and having a mechanism to revert to a previous version if something goes wrong. In a Rust environment, this could involve simply keeping previous binaries and their corresponding model files, or in more advanced scenarios, using container orchestration systems like Kubernetes that manage versioning automatically.

Every stage, from deciding on a deployment plan to keeping an eye on the deployed model, comes with its own unique set of issues and obstacles. To ensure your model goes from being used in a research setting to making predictions in the real world, it is important to understand these processes thoroughly.

Summary

The main emphasis of this chapter was to develop and deploy a Rust-based linear regression model. Root Mean Square Error (RMSE), Coefficient of Determination (R-squared), and Mean Absolute Error (MAE) are some of the metrics that we extensively covered in our initial learning on the significance of evaluating a machine learning model. We can fine-tune the model for optimal results with the use of these measures, which give a nuanced insight of its performance. We also looked at residual plots to see if they could be useful for evaluating models qualitatively. We were able to get a full picture of the model's predictive ability by integrating these quantitative and qualitative approaches.

You can save a trained model to a JSON file and then reload it to make fresh predictions. The Serde library introduced the concept of model serialization. Both the sharing of models and their deployment depend on this. We demonstrated how to package a trained machine learning model for deployment or further usage by learning about how to write and read this serialized model to a file.

Next, we dove into the implementation details, going over various ways to make the model available as a web service or as an integral part of a Rust program. Optional processes for encapsulating the model in an online service utilizing Rocket or Actix frameworks were part of this. The importance of post-deployment tasks like monitoring and logging in keeping a machine learning system running well in a production setting was also emphasized.

The need of a minimal deployment strategy was highlighted as we wrapped up by going over more advanced topics like versioning and rollback procedures. This chapter provided a comprehensive overview of the whole process, from model evaluation to deployment, and presented practical insights and strategies that may be used in real-world machine learning projects that are based on Rust.

CHAPTER 4: LOGISTIC REGRESSION FOR CLASSIFICATION

Overview

Linear regression serves as a foundational stone in the realm of supervised learning, especially for continuous outcomes. It is often the starting point for predictive modeling and offers a linear relationship between the dependent and independent variables. With its simplicity, it is best suited for problems where the relationship between the variables is approximately linear and doesn't require capturing complex nonlinear patterns. Although powerful, the scope of linear regression is confined to predicting numeric values. That is where logistic regression comes into play, broadening the horizon to classification problems.

Logistic regression is fundamentally different from its linear counterpart in what it aims to predict. While linear regression is designed to output continuous values, logistic regression focuses on binary outcomes—things like 'Yes' or 'No,' 'True' or 'False,' '1' or '0'. The output of a logistic regression model is a probability that the given input belongs to a particular class, which is transformed into a binary outcome via a threshold (e.g., if the output probability is greater than 0.5, classify as class '1'). This makes it highly valuable in fields like healthcare for disease prediction, in finance for credit scoring, and in marketing for customer churn prediction.

The magic behind logistic regression lies in its utilization of the logistic function, also known as the sigmoid function. Unlike the linear function used in linear regression, the sigmoid function maps any input into a value between 0 and 1, making it suitable for a probability estimate. This sigmoid function is what differentiates logistic regression and allows it to handle classification problems effectively. The curve of the sigmoid function is S-shaped, and as it approaches infinity, the predicted value clings to 1; as it approaches negative infinity, the predicted value comes close to 0.

What's even more compelling is logistic regression's ability to work with multiple predictor variables, both numerical and categorical. It can also handle more complex scenarios through techniques like regularization, which helps prevent overfitting. This means that logistic regression isn't just a simple linear separator; it can adapt to data with some level of complexity while maintaining its inherent simplicity and interpretability. This makes it easier to understand the impact of individual features on the prediction, a property that is often vital in areas like healthcare and social sciences where interpretability is crucial.

Logistic regression has its limitations, such as the assumption of linearity between the dependent variable and the independent variables. It also requires that the observations are independent of each other, which is not the case in sequences and time series data. However, despite these limitations, it remains a robust and widely-used algorithm due to its efficiency and ease of interpretation. It serves as a stepping stone to more complex algorithms like Decision Trees, Random Forests, and Neural Networks, but it holds its own ground firmly, especially when the problem at hand doesn't require capturing complex relationships and patterns.

Introduction to Logistic Regression

After you've loaded and preprocessed your data, you may begin the logistic regression modeling technique. The first and possibly most important phase is feature selection. Even though logistic regression is less sensitive to irrelevant information than some other algorithms, effective feature selection can significantly enhance model performance. Recursive Feature Elimination (RFE), Lasso regularization, and simple correlation matrices are also suitable feature selection strategies in these circumstances. Youmay do correlation calculations manually or with libraries that provide feature selection methods. The chosen traits should be both statistically significant and domain-appropriate.

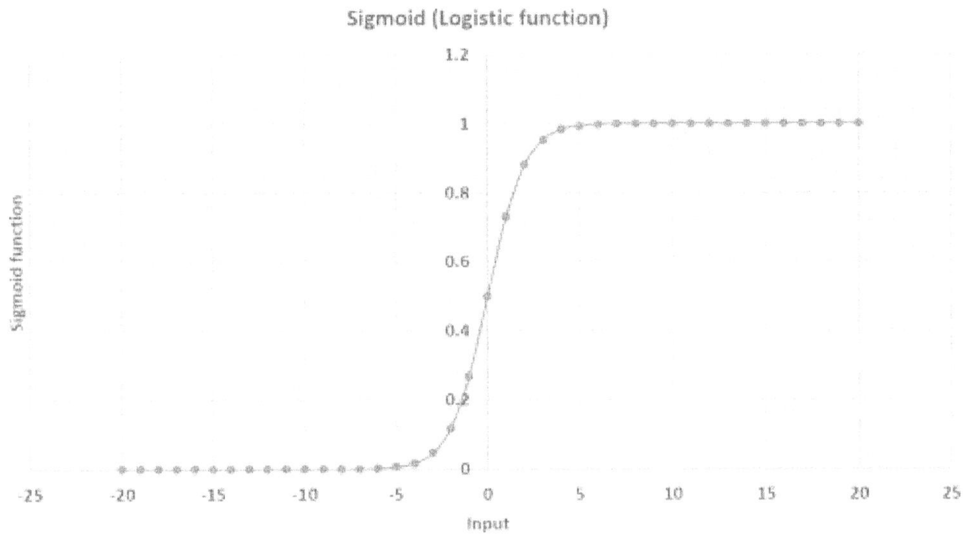

Fig 4.1 Logistic Regression Overview

The next step after feature selection is to divide your dataset into training and testing sets. This allows you to evaluate the model's performance on previously unseen data later. While Rust lacks a direct equivalent to scikit-learn's train_test_split function in Python, random sampling methods can provide the same functionality. For example, you can shuffle your dataset before manually dividing it into training and testing groups using a ratio of 80-20 or 70-30, respectively. Ensuring a good split is critical for model evaluation since an imbalanced or skewed split might result in inaccurate performance indicators.

After the data has been separated, you may start training the model. Logistic regression, like linear regression, aims to identify the best-fitting parameters. However, rather than utilizing basic least squares, logistic regression often uses maximum likelihood estimation (MLE) to determine these parameters. Several Rust libraries, like linfa and smartcore, provide logistic regression functionality. During training, the algorithm iteratively modifies the weights assigned to each of your features to minimize a loss function, thereby "learning" from the training data. The end result is a set of weights that can be used to predict fresh data.

After the model has been trained, the next stage is to make predictions on test data. The logistic function converts these predictions to probability. These probabilities can be converted into binary class labels by setting a threshold value, which is commonly 0.5. The prediction phase would be to load the trained model, apply it to the test data, and generate probabilities using the logistic function. The probabilities are then converted to class labels using a simple function based on the threshold specified.

After predictions are made, model evaluation begins. Unlike linear regression, which utilizes RMSE or R-squared, logistic regression frequently employs additional measures such as accuracy, precision, recall, and the F1-score. Confusion matrices are also widely used to assess the effectiveness of classification methods. These metrics give you a complete picture of how well your model is performing in terms of both false positives and false negatives. Libraries such as evcxr can help you calculate these metrics.

The final stage in logistic regression modeling is usually hyperparameter adjustment. The most common hyperparameter in logistic regression is regularization strength, which can help prevent overfitting. Grid search and random search methods can be used to identify the best hyperparameters. Once the optimal hyperparameters have been identified, the model can be retrained on the full dataset using these optimized settings.

The above steps will help you create a strong logistic regression model. The method includes several stages, each with its own set of obstacles and considerations, ranging from feature selection to model evaluation and tuning. Understanding each step can help you develop a good logistic regression model while also laying the groundwork for more sophisticated methods.

Implement Logistic Regression

Now that we have the heart attack prediction dataset, we apply logistic regression to it. Our target variable will be a binary result that indicates whether or not a heart attack is likely to occur. We will use feature data such as age, gender, and cholesterol levels to forecast this outcome.

Problem Statement and Data Splitting

The stated objective of applying logistic regression is to ascertain the probability of a patient experiencing a heart attack. For this, we will utilize a binary classification: '1' for likely, '0' for unlikely. Because we've previously preprocessed the data, we will proceed to dividing it into training and testing sets. The Rust standard library includes methods for shuffling a vector. Once shuffled, divide the vector into two independent vectors for training and testing. We assume an 80-20 split ratio, which means that 80% of the data will be used for training and 20% for testing.

Model Training

You will call a `fit` or `train` method to train the model on your training data. During this training phase, the algorithm will initialize a set of weights for each feature and iteratively adjust these weights using a method like gradient descent to minimize a loss function. Since we're doing this in Rust, the math would be implemented in low-level code, involving a fair amount of linear algebra. You would use libraries like `ndarray` for matrix operations to compute the gradient and update the weights.

Making Predictions

Once the model is trained, you will use it to make predictions on your test data. The logistic function will transform these raw predictions into probabilities. Then you will apply a threshold, commonly 0.5, to classify these probabilities into the binary classes '1' or '0'. This would typically involve a `predict` function that takes in your test data and returns the predictions. The logistic function `1 / (1 + e^-value)` can be easily implemented to convert these predictions to probabilities.

Evaluation Metrics

After predictions, evaluating the model's performance is crucial. For logistic regression, commonly used metrics include accuracy, precision, recall, and the F1 score. Confusion matrices are also a robust way to see how the model performs in terms of false positives and false negatives. You would write functions to compute these metrics manually. You will compare the model's predictions with the actual outcomes in the test data to compute these metrics. For instance, accuracy can be calculated as the number of correct predictions, divided by total predictions.

Hyperparameter Tuning

The final step is usually to tune hyperparameters such as regularization strength and learning rate to improve the model's performance. In a larger ecosystem, hyperparameter tweaking may often be accomplished using methods such as grid search or random search. You may use a simple loop to go through a set of hyperparameters, retrain the model, and assess its performance using cross-validation. The hyperparameters that produce the best results would then be utilized to retrain the model on the whole dataset.

The above steps will allow you to train, predict, and assess a logistic regression model. While languages like Python provide more comprehensive machine learning APIs, Rust's emphasis on safety and performance makes it a compelling alternative for developing ML algorithms from the ground up.

Performance Metrics Deep Dive

After you've trained your logistic regression model and generated predictions on your test data, looking into performance metrics is critical for assessing the model's success. In addition to measuring your model's performance, the metrics disclose the types of errors it is making. Accuracy, precision, recall, and the F1 score are frequently the most useful measures for forecasting the chance of a heart attack in a binary classification problem like ours. Furthermore, the Receiver Operating Characteristic (ROC) curve and the area under this curve (AUC-ROC) are useful for determining the model's performance at various threshold levels. These indicators are not mutually exclusive, but rather complementing, offering several viewpoints on the model's success.

Understanding Accuracy

Accuracy refers to the proportion of true positives and true negatives in all predictions. It is the most straightforward statistic, but it can be deceptive, particularly in skewed datasets. For example, if 95% of patients are unlikely to have a heart attack, a naive model forecasting that no one will have a heart attack will still be 95% correct. Accuracy is calculated as the number of correct predictions divided by the total number of guesses. While accuracy is an excellent starting point, it is rarely sufficient for a thorough assessment of your model's performance.

Precision and Recall

Precision is defined as the ratio of true positives to the sum of true and false positives. It responds to the query, "Of all the patients the model predicted are likely to have a heart attack, how many actually did?" The proportion of correct results to the total number of correct and incorrect results is known as recall or sensitivity. It replies to the question, "Of all the patients who actually had a heart attack, how many did the model correctly predict?" These measurements are especially relevant when the costs of false positives and false negatives are dramatically different. In our example, a false negative—a patient who is likely to suffer a heart attack but is forecast otherwise—could be fatal.

F1 Score and Confusion Matrix

The F1 score is the harmonic mean of precision and recall, resulting in a single statistic that accounts for both false positives and false negatives. An F1 score achieves its maximum value at 1 (perfect precision and recall) and its lowest at 0. A confusion matrix, on the other hand, provides a tabular representation of Actual vs. Predicted values as well as information on false positives, false negatives, true positives, and true negatives. This allows you to understand the model's performance from many perspectives and, if necessary, manually calculate other measures.

ROC Curve and AUC-ROC

The Receiver Operating Characteristic (ROC) curve is a graphical representation of a classification model's performance across various categorization thresholds. The graph shows the True Positive Rate (Recall) versus the False Positive Rate. The area under the ROC curve (AUC-ROC) is an aggregate measure of the model's performance at all classification criteria. An AUC-ROC score of one implies complete predictive capacity, whereas 0.5 shows no predictive power. To plot these, adjust the decision threshold and calculate the True Positive and False Positive rates for each.

Comparing Metrics

Finally, the metrics should be consistent with the original problem statement. For predicting heart attacks, good recall may be more significant than high precision because false negatives might be fatal. Depending on what the healthcare provider emphasizes, you may need to modify the model or collect additional variables to improve specific KPIs. These measures should also be compared to a baseline model, such as one that makes random guesses, to determine whether your model improves predictive power.

Model Hyperparameter Tuning Process

After evaluating the model's performance using various metrics, the next step is hyperparameter tuning. Hyperparameters are external configurations for an algorithm that are not learned from the data. They are constant parameters whose values are set prior to the machine learning process. For logistic regression, the most commonly tuned hyperparameter is the regularization strength, often denoted by λ or C, where $C=1/\lambda$.

Regularization can help prevent overfitting by adding a penalty term to the loss function that the algorithm optimizes. Other hyperparameters could include the learning rate for optimization algorithms like gradient descent, or the type of regularization used (L1, L2, or Elastic Net).

Grid Search Methodology

One common method for hyperparameter tuning is grid search. In grid search, you define a set of possible values for each hyperparameter you want to tune. The algorithm then tries every possible combination of these hyperparameters and returns the set that gives the best performance according to a metric you choose, such as F1-score or accuracy. In the Rust programming environment, you could implement grid search by nesting loops for each hyperparameter, training a new model for each iteration with the given hyperparameter set, and storing the performance of each model.

Random Search Methodology

Another approach for hyperparameter tuning is random search, where you randomly sample hyperparameters from a distribution over the possible parameter values. This method is more computationally efficient than grid search and has been shown to yield equally good results in less time. You could use the `rand` library to generate random numbers for each hyperparameter according to the chosen distribution, be it uniform or something more complex like Gaussian.

Cross-Validation in Tuning

When using either grid search or random search, it is crucial to use cross-validation to get an unbiased estimate of the model's performance with each set of hyperparameters. Cross-validation involves splitting the training data into k subsets. The model is trained on $k-1$ of these subsets and validated on the remaining one. This process is repeated k times with each subset used exactly once for validation. The k results are then averaged to get a single performance metric. This would involve manually implementing the data splitting, model training, and evaluation steps within the hyperparameter tuning loop.

Fine-Tuning and Iterative Process

Once you've identified the best hyperparameters using grid search or random search, you might want to perform a more localized search around these values. This fine-tuning can sometimes yield small but significant improvements in model performance. Moreover, hyperparameter tuning is often an iterative process. You might start with a broad range of values and then narrow it down based on initial results. Alternatively, you may discover that adding or removing features affects the optimal hyperparameters, necessitating another round of tuning.

Final Model Training and Verification

After identifying the best hyperparameters, the final step is to retrain the model using these optimized settings on the entire training dataset. This model is what you would typically deploy or use for making further predictions. However, before proceeding to deployment, it is crucial to evaluate this final model on the test dataset to verify that it performs.

Sample Program: Hyperparameter Tuning

For example, let us consider a simplified version of grid search and cross-validation, implemented in following steps:

Define Hyperparameter Space and Cross-Validation

Firstly, define the range of hyperparameters you want to explore. We consider regularization strengths λ in the set $\{0.001, 0.01, 0.1, 1\}$ and learning rates α in the set $\{0.001, 0.01, 0.1\}$.

```
let regularization_strengths = vec![0.001, 0.01, 0.1, 1.0];

let learning_rates = vec![0.001, 0.01, 0.1];
```

For a simplified 3-fold cross-validation, manually split your training data into three parts. Train the model on two parts and validate it on the remaining part, cycling through all combinations.

Grid Search Loop

Next, iterate over all combinations of λ and α to train models and evaluate their performance using cross-validation. Store the performance metrics for each.

```
let mut best_f1 = 0.0;

let mut best_params = (0.0, 0.0);


for &reg_strength in &regularization_strengths {

 for &learning_rate in &learning_rates {

 let mut avg_f1_score = 0.0;

  // Here goes your model training and validation code

 // Update avg_f1_score based on the F1 score of the validation set

  if avg_f1_score > best_f1 {

 best_f1 = avg_f1_score;

 best_params = (reg_strength, learning_rate);

 }

 }

}
```

Train and Evaluate the Model

After identifying the best hyperparameters, train the model using these on the entire training set. Then, you can use this model to make predictions on the test set and evaluate its performance to ensure it generalizes well to unseen data.

With these above steps, you can systematically tune the hyperparameters for a logistic regression model implemented, assess its performance, and ensure that you are using the most robust model for making future predictions.

Serialize and Deserialize the Model

Now that you've fine-tuned your logistic regression model, the next logical step is to save it for future use. This involves serializing the model into a format that can be easily stored and later loaded. Serialization can be performed using libraries like `serde`. We assume that your logistic regression model has two main components to serialize: the weights and the bias. These can be encapsulated into a struct:

```
#[derive(Serialize, Deserialize)]

struct LogisticRegressionModel {

 weights: Vec<f64>,

 bias: f64,

}
```

To serialize this struct into a JSON file, you can use `serde_json`, an extension of `serde` for JSON serialization:

```
use serde_json::to_string_pretty;

let model = LogisticRegressionModel {

 weights: vec![...], // Your trained weights here

 bias: ..., // Your trained bias here

};

let serialized_model = to_string_pretty(&model).expect("Failed to serialize model");
```

After serializing, save this JSON string to a file:

```
use std::fs::File;

use std::io::prelude::*;

let mut file = File::create("logistic_model.json").expect("Could not create file");
```

```
file.write_all(serialized_model.as_bytes()).expect("Could not write to file");
```

Similarly, you can deserialize the JSON back into a **LogisticRegressionModel** struct using **serde_json**. Given below is how you read the JSON string from the file and convert it back into a model:

```
use std::fs::read_to_string;

use serde_json::from_str;

let serialized_model = read_to_string("logistic_model.json").expect("Could not read
file");

let deserialized_model: LogisticRegressionModel =
from_str(&serialized_model).expect("Failed to deserialize");
```

Once deserialized, you can then use this model for making predictions, exactly as you would with the model object you originally trained.

```
// Assume `predict` is a function that takes LogisticRegressionModel, and input features
to make a prediction

let prediction = predict(&deserialized_model, &input_features);
```

While performing serialization and deserialization, there are some considerations to keep in mind. One is security: ensure that the serialized model is stored in a secure location, especially if it contains sensitive data. Another is versioning: if you update the model structure (e.g., adding more features or layers), ensure that you version serialized models so that you can still load older models if needed.

Summary

In this chapter, we explored logistic regression, an essential algorithm in machine learning for classification problems. Beginning with the theoretical foundations, we investigated how logistic regression predicts the probability of a binary outcome as a function of the independent variables. The logistic function, also known as the sigmoid function, is crucial to this approach, converting linear combinations of information into a value between 0 and 1, which is then interpreted as the likelihood of the positive class. We also discussed hyperparameter tuning, which involves optimizing regularization and learning rates to generate the best effective model.

We next moved on to more practical components, such as data preparation and model training. We learned how to use logistic regression on a heart attack prediction dataset. We completed the full cycle of model training, validation, and evaluation. Hyperparameter tweaking was carried out via grid search, which involved iteratively training the model with various hyperparameter combinations and evaluating it using cross-validation. This iterative method helped discover the best model settings, which were then utilized to train the final model.

Additionally, the chapter covered the serialization and deserialization processes, which are vital following model training. These methods allow you to save a trained model to a file and then reload it for future predictions. We learned how to use Rust libraries such as serde to perform these actions. By serializing the model, we can avoid the retraining step in subsequent challenges, saving time and processing resources. This is especially useful for deploying models in live applications where fast predictions are frequently required.

The purpose of this chapter was to provide a thorough understanding of logistic regression in both theory and practice, demonstrating how to implement, analyze, and optimize a logistic regression model.

CHAPTER 5: DECISION TREES IN ACTION

Introduction to Decision Trees

Decision trees are one of the most straightforward yet powerful algorithms in the machine learning landscape. At their core, decision trees work by breaking down a complex decision-making process into a series of simpler decisions, thereby providing a solution that is both understandable and actionable. The algorithm constructs a tree where each node represents a feature in the dataset, each branch represents a decision rule, and each leaf node represents the outcome. The root of the tree is the feature that best splits the dataset into classes based on a chosen metric like Gini impurity or information gain.

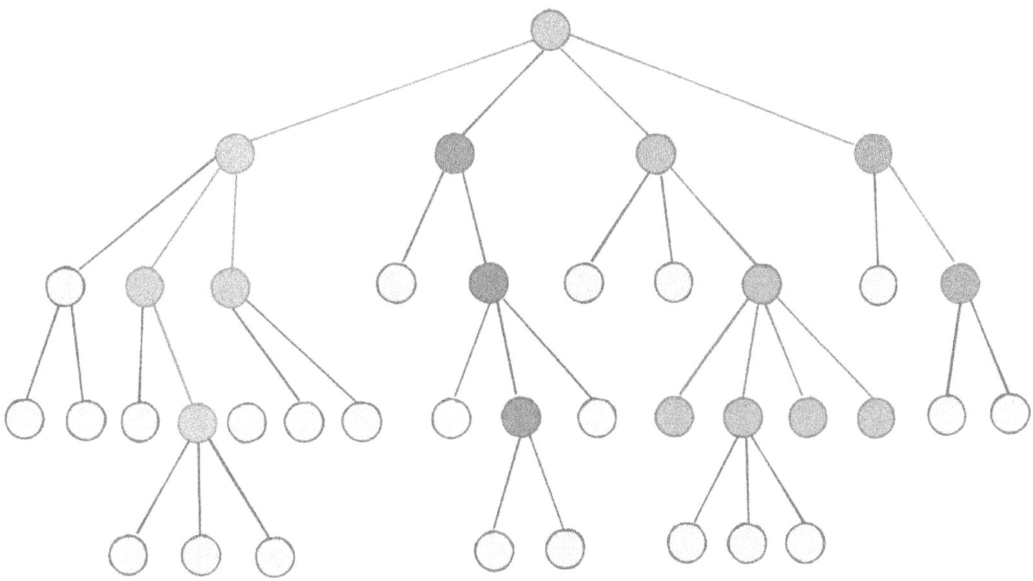

Fig 5.1 Decision Tree Overview

Interpretable and Transparent Model

One of the most appealing characteristics of decision trees is their interpretability. Unlike many machine learning models that are often considered "black boxes," decision trees provide a transparent model structure that can be visualized and understood. This is particularly beneficial in sectors like healthcare, finance, and law, where being able to explain a model's predictions is not just advantageous but sometimes legally required. For instance, in a medical diagnosis application, a decision tree can provide both the prediction and the logical steps leading to that prediction, allowing medical professionals to understand the basis for a machine-generated diagnosis.

Feature Importance and Selection

Decision trees have a built-in feature selection, identifying the most important variables early in the tree, thus eliminating the need for separate feature selection procedures. In many cases, less informative variables will not even appear in the tree, making it both efficient and effective at handling high-dimensional data. This aspect has significantly contributed to their application in various domains like genomics, where high-dimensional data is the norm. Researchers and data scientists can focus on those critical variables for further studies or data collection, saving time and resources.

Handling Categorical and Numerical Data

Another innovation brought by decision trees is the ability to handle both categorical and numerical data natively. Many machine learning algorithms require that all data be numeric, but decision trees can split data based on categories just as easily as they can split them based on numeric thresholds. This flexibility makes decision trees extremely versatile and widely applicable, reducing the need for cumbersome data preprocessing steps like one-hot encoding or normalization.

Ensemble Methods and Random Forests

The impact of decision trees extends beyond individual models, serving as the basis for ensemble methods like Random Forests and Gradient Boosting Trees. These ensemble methods combine multiple decision trees to create a more robust and accurate model, effectively overcoming some of the limitations of a single tree, such as overfitting. In Random Forests, for example, multiple trees are built on different subsets of the data, and their predictions are averaged (for regression) or voted upon (for classification) to produce the final output. This innovation has significantly advanced the field, offering a balance between performance and interpretability.

Decision trees are highly adaptable and have seen widespread adoption in various practical applications ranging from credit scoring and customer segmentation to natural language processing and computer vision. Their simplicity and versatility make them an excellent choice for embedded systems and real-time analytics, where computational resources may be limited. In these scenarios, a well-tuned decision tree can offer performance comparable to more complex models but with the advantage of faster inference times and lower memory requirements. Through these features and innovations, decision trees have carved a niche for themselves as one of the go-to algorithms for a wide range of machine learning tasks. Their ability to provide interpretable, efficient, and versatile models makes them indispensable in the evolving landscape of machine learning and artificial intelligence.

Online Purchase Retail Dataset

A lot of businesses in the retail sector utilize this sort of dataset to learn about their customers' likes and dislikes, which helps them with things like inventory optimization, personalizing marketing, and making customers happier. The dataset is available in the following URL: https://www.kaggle.com/datasets/yasserh/customer-segmentation-dataset/data

The dataset contains multiple attributes such as:

1. CustomerID: A unique identifier for each customer.
2. InvoiceNo: The invoice number, which is a unique identifier for each transaction.
3. StockCode: The product code for the item purchased.
4. Description: A text description of the item.
5. Quantity: The number of items purchased in the transaction.
6. InvoiceDate: The date and time when the purchase was made.
7. UnitPrice: The price of a single unit of the item.
8. Country: The country where the customer resides.

Each of the above attributes plays a crucial role, like:

- CustomerID and InvoiceNo serve as identifiers that can be used for aggregating data at the customer or transaction level.
- StockCode and Description provide insights into what items are popular among customers.
- Quantity and UnitPrice are directly related to revenue and can be used to calculate metrics like average order value.
- InvoiceDate could be useful for time-based analyses like seasonality or cohort analysis.
- Country can be useful for geographic segmentation or to analyze regional trends.
- Given the attributes, there are numerous analytical possibilities:
- Customer Segmentation: Using attributes like Quantity and UnitPrice, customers could be segmented into different groups like high-value vs. low-value customers.
- Product Analysis: The StockCode and Description fields could be used for product-based analyses to determine which items are the most popular or generate the most revenue.
- Time-Series Analysis: The InvoiceDate field allows for a range of time-based analyses, including seasonality effects and trends over time.
- Geographic Analysis: The Country attribute could be used to perform geographic segmentation, identifying specific countries or regions that contribute significantly to revenue or customer engagement.

Given its rich set of attributes, this dataset offers a wide range of possibilities for analysis and model training, and hence we will use it in this chapter related to decision trees implementation and furthermore.

Data Processing for Decision Trees

Reading the Excel File and Initial Exploration

Before diving into data preprocessing, the first step is to read the Excel dataset into a Rust DataFrame. You can utilize the **polars** library for this task. It's important to inspect the first few rows and the data types of each column. This initial exploration will give you insights into what kind of preprocessing steps are needed. For example, you might observe that some columns contain missing values, or that numerical columns are interpreted as strings. Such preliminary inspection helps in outlining the preprocessing steps.

```
use polars::prelude::*;

fn read_excel_to_df(file_path: &str) -> Result<DataFrame> {

 let file = std::fs::File::open(file_path)?;

 let reader = ReaderBuilder::new().from_reader(file);

 let df = reader.finish()?;

 Ok(df)

}
```

Handling Missing Values

After initial inspection, you may find that some columns have missing values. Missing data can be problematic because decision tree algorithms generally do not handle missing values natively. Therefore, you have to decide whether to remove rows with missing values or fill them with a specific value. Each approach has its pros and cons. Removing rows could lead to loss of data, while filling missing values could introduce bias. You can use **polars** to fill missing values in a column with the mean, median, or a constant value.

```
let df = df.fill_none("ColumnName", FillNoneStrategy::Mean)?;
```

Encoding Categorical Variables

If your dataset contains categorical variables, they need to be converted into a numerical format with a common technique of label encoding, where each unique category in a column is mapped to an integer. This encoding can be done easily using polars by converting the categorical column into a 'UInt32' type.

```
let df = df.cast(&["ColumnName"], DataType::UInt32)?;
```

Data Splitting

Once the data is cleaned and prepared, it is time to split it into training and testing sets. The training set is used to build the decision tree model, while the testing set is used to evaluate its performance. The polars library allows you to randomly split a DataFrame into two separate sets.

```
let (train_df, test_df) = df.rand_split(0.8);
```

Data Normalization

While decision trees generally don't require feature scaling, it can be beneficial in some scenarios. For example, if you plan to visualize the data or use the decision tree as part of an ensemble method that does require scaling, then it makes sense to normalize the features. The polars library can be used to scale a column to have zero mean and unit variance.

```
let df = df.with_column(

 (col("ColumnName") - mean) / stddev

)?;
```

These data processing steps confirm that the dataset is in the right format and condition for applying the decision tree algorithm.

Performing Feature Extraction

Creating Customer Lifetime Value

One of the most impactful features in retail analytics is Customer Lifetime Value (CLV), which represents the total revenue a customer is expected to generate over the course of their relationship with a business. In our "Online Purchase Retail" dataset, you could calculate a rudimentary form of CLV by summing up the 'TotalPrice' (i.e., 'Quantity' multiplied by 'UnitPrice') for each customer. This can be a valuable feature for the decision tree, as it gives an overall picture of customer worth. You can use the **groupby** and **agg** functions of the **polars** library to achieve this.

```
let df = df.groupby("CustomerID").agg(&[

 col("TotalPrice").sum().alias("CustomerLifetimeValue")

])?;
```

Temporal Feature Engineering

The 'InvoiceDate' field can be a treasure trove of temporal features. You can extract the day of the week, month, quarter, or even the hour of the day when most purchases occur. These features could reveal interesting patterns, like higher purchases over weekends or during holiday seasons, and add layers of understanding to the decision tree model. For example, you could create a new feature representing whether a purchase was made on a weekend.

```
let df = df.with_column(

 when(col("InvoiceDayOfWeek").eq(6)).or(col("InvoiceDayOfWeek").eq(7))

 .then(1)

 .otherwise(0)

 .alias("IsWeekendPurchase")

)?;
```

Average Purchase Value

Another interesting feature could be the average purchase value for each customer. This is simply the total spend of the customer divided by the number of transactions they have made. This can provide insights into spending habits on a per-transaction basis, which can be a useful metric for segmentation.

```
let df = df.groupby("CustomerID").agg(&[
```

```
(col("TotalPrice").sum() / col("InvoiceNo").count()).alias("AvgPurchaseValue")

])?;
```

Seasonality Features

Considering retail data often shows seasonality, you might want to encode information about typical high and low seasons for sales. For instance, you could create a binary feature indicating whether a purchase was made in a high season based on historical sales data.

```
let df = df.with_column(

 when(col("InvoiceMonth").eq(11)).or(col("InvoiceMonth").eq(12))

 .then(1)

 .otherwise(0)

 .alias("HighSeasonPurchase")

)?;
```

Product Categories

If the 'Description' or 'StockCode' fields contain information that allows you to classify products into broader categories, this could be another powerful feature. For instance, electronic items and clothing could be different categories. These categories can be used to understand customer preferences at a broader level, making it easier for the decision tree to split nodes based on customer behavior. You might need to manually map 'StockCode' or 'Description' to categories, but once done, it can be encoded like other categorical variables.

```
let df = df.with_column(

 when(col("StockCode").lt(5000)).then("Electronics")

 .when(col("StockCode").lt(10000)).then("Clothing")

 .otherwise("Other")

 .alias("ProductCategory")
```

```
)?;
```

Geographical Features

The 'Country' field can be engineered further to indicate the geographical region rather than just the country. For example, "USA," "Canada," and "Mexico" could be grouped under 'North America'. This broad classification can help if certain behaviors or trends are regional rather than country-specific.

```
let df = df.with_column(

when(col("Country").eq("USA")).or(col("Country").eq("Canada")).or(col("Country").eq("
Mexico"))

 .then("North America")

 .otherwise("OtherRegion")

 .alias("Region")

)?;
```

The dataset we're building using these feature engineering techniques will supply the model with raw data as well as rich derived features that capture customer behavior from many perspectives. This complete dataset is now ready to be used to train a decision tree model, as we will see in the coming section.

Initialize and Train Decision Trees

So far, we have created features such as 'CustomerLifetimeValue', 'IsWeekendPurchase', 'AvgPurchaseValue', 'HighSeasonPurchase', and 'Region' as learned earlier.

Separate Features and Labels

First, you can separate the dataset into features (X) and labels (y). In our case, we say we are interested in predicting 'HighSeasonPurchase' based on other features. You would extract this column as your labels and use the rest as features. Do not forget to split your data into training and testing sets.

```
let (train_df, test_df) = df.rand_split(0.8);

let x_train: Array2<f64> = train_df.select_at_idx([1, 2, 3,
4]).unwrap().to_ndarray().unwrap();

let y_train: Array1<f64> =
train_df.column("HighSeasonPurchase").unwrap().to_ndarray().unwrap();
```

Initialize Decision Tree Model

You would typically define a struct to represent the decision tree and its nodes. Each node would contain information like the feature to split on, the threshold for the split, and the left and right children.

```
struct DecisionNode {

 feature_index: usize,

 threshold: f64,

 left: Box<DecisionNode>,

 right: Box<DecisionNode>,

 is_leaf: bool,

 value: Option<f64>,

}
```

Training the Model

Training the model involves recursively partitioning the data by selecting the feature that provides the best split. The best split is often determined by calculating the Gini impurity or information gain after each potential split and selecting the one that maximizes this metric.

Following is a recursive function to train the tree:

```
impl DecisionNode {

 fn train(&mut self, x_train: Array2<f64>, y_train: Array1<f64>) {
```

```
if some_stopping_condition {
self.is_leaf = true;
self.value = Some(calculate_leaf_value(y_train));
return;
}
let (best_feature, best_threshold) = find_best_split(x_train, y_train);
let (x_left, x_right, y_left, y_right) = split_data(x_train, y_train, best_feature,
best_threshold);
self.feature_index = best_feature;
self.threshold = best_threshold;
self.left = Box::new(DecisionNode::new());
self.left.train(x_left, y_left);
self.right = Box::new(DecisionNode::new());
self.right.train(x_right, y_right);
}
}
```

Model Evaluation

Once the tree is trained, you can use it to make predictions on the test set. Walk through each data point down the tree, following the left or right child based on whether the feature at the node's feature_index is below or above the node's threshold.

After obtaining predictions, you can evaluate the model's performance using metrics such as accuracy, precision, and recall.

```
let y_pred = test_df.map_rows(|row| {
```

```
let mut node = &trained_tree_root;

while !node.is_leaf {

let feature_value = row[node.feature_index];

node = if feature_value < node.threshold { &node.left } else { &node.right };

}

node.value.unwrap()

});
```

Making Predictions

Once your decision tree model is trained, making predictions involves traversing the tree with your test or new data points. You start at the root and make decisions based on the feature values of the data point until you reach a leaf node. The value at the leaf node will be the model's prediction for that data point.

Given below is how to use a trained decision tree for predictions:

```
impl DecisionNode {

pub fn predict(&self, x: Array1<f64>) -> f64 {

if self.is_leaf {

return self.value.unwrap();

}

let feature_value = x[self.feature_index];

if feature_value < self.threshold {

return self.left.predict(x);

} else {

return self.right.predict(x);
```

```
}
}
}
```

In the above function, x is a single row of features you want to predict the label for. We start at the root (self in this case is the root), and go left or right depending on whether the value of the feature at feature_index is less than threshold. This process is repeated recursively until a leaf node is reached, at which point the value at the leaf node is returned as the prediction.

Batch Predictions

We usually have multiple data points (rows) for which you want to make predictions. You would loop through your test data to get individual predictions for each row.

```
let mut y_pred: Vec<f64> = Vec::new();

for row in x_test.outer_iter() {

 let prediction = trained_tree_root.predict(row);

 y_pred.push(prediction);

}
```

In the above code snippet, x_test would be a 2D array where each row is a set of features for a data point in your test set. We iterate through each row in x_test, make a prediction using our trained decision tree, and store it in y_pred.

Model Interpretation

One of the biggest advantages of decision trees is their interpretability. Each decision made by the tree corresponds to a real-world feature, making it easy to understand why a particular prediction was made. By examining the features and thresholds at each node, you can gain insights into what factors most influence the model's predictions.

After making predictions, the next logical steps would usually involve evaluating the model's performance using metrics like accuracy, precision, and recall. This evaluation would give you a numerical measure of how well your model is performing and might prompt you to go back to the feature engineering or model training stages to make improvements. Whether we are classifying customer segments or predicting sales, the steps remain fundamentally the same. The skills you've gained here are transferable to many other machine learning algorithms and practical scenarios.

Summary

Beginning with an overview of the method and its effects on ML projects, this chapter dove headfirst into the world of Decision Trees. We learned how Decision Trees help to create a more interpretable and flexible modeling approach capable of handling both classification and regression challenges. The algorithm's unique capacity to emulate human decision-making by making hierarchical decisions based on attributes makes it highly adaptable and intelligible, giving a clear picture of how predictions are made.

We then moved on to a hands-on use of Decision Trees in Rust. The primary focus was on understanding the structure of a decision tree using Rust's struct and iteratively training it to produce splits depending on features and thresholds. This approach, albeit laborious, provided a detailed grasp of the model's underlying workings, from feature selection for splitting to leaf node generation. We not only defined and trained the model, but we also learnt how to create batch predictions using the decision tree, which solidified our comprehension of this useful approach.

The feature engineering phase was especially interesting. We altered our Online Retail dataset to generate additional characteristics that capture various elements of consumer behavior, including consumer Lifetime Value, purchase timing, and regional segmentation. These constructed features provided additional depth to our model, allowing it to make more accurate and insightful predictions. We used Rust's Polars library extensively throughout this step, taking advantage of its quick DataFrame functions to manage and prepare our dataset.

Finally, we practiced making predictions using our trained model. Each data point moved through the tree from root to leaf, making a choice based on a feature and a threshold. This journey through the tree's decision-making stages ended in a leaf node, which contained the final forecast. The entire process was carried out in Rust, giving us significant hands-on experience with implementing machine learning algorithms in a systems programming language. This comprehensive grasp of decision trees, together with the practical skills learned, provides a sufficient foundation for delving into more sophisticated ensemble approaches, such as Random Forests, in subsequent chapters.

Chapter 6: Mastering Random Forests

Introduction to Random Forests

Random Forests might be viewed of as the "wisdom of the crowd" in the machine learning world. They are an ensemble learning method that extends the concept of a single decision tree by integrating many trees to produce more accurate and robust predictions. Instead of depending on one tree's decision-making powers, a Random Forest uses the collective intelligence of a 'ensemble' of trees. Each tree in the ensemble is trained on a separate subset of the data, and when it comes to making a forecast, the forest casts a vote, with the majority winning. This approach captures the spirit of ensemble learning, which is all about combining numerous weaker models to create a single powerful model.

Ensemble learning and Random Forests have a strong link. The name 'ensemble' literally means 'group,' and in machine learning, ensemble methods such as Random Forests, Gradient Boosting, and AdaBoost combine numerous models to increase overall performance. Random Forests' ensemble concept enables the "democratization" of decision-making processes. It's similar to how a jury's collective decision is more balanced and fair than a single juror. Random Forests lessen the risk of overfitting, which is typical with single decision trees. Each tree records distinct patterns, and their combination yields a more generic model.

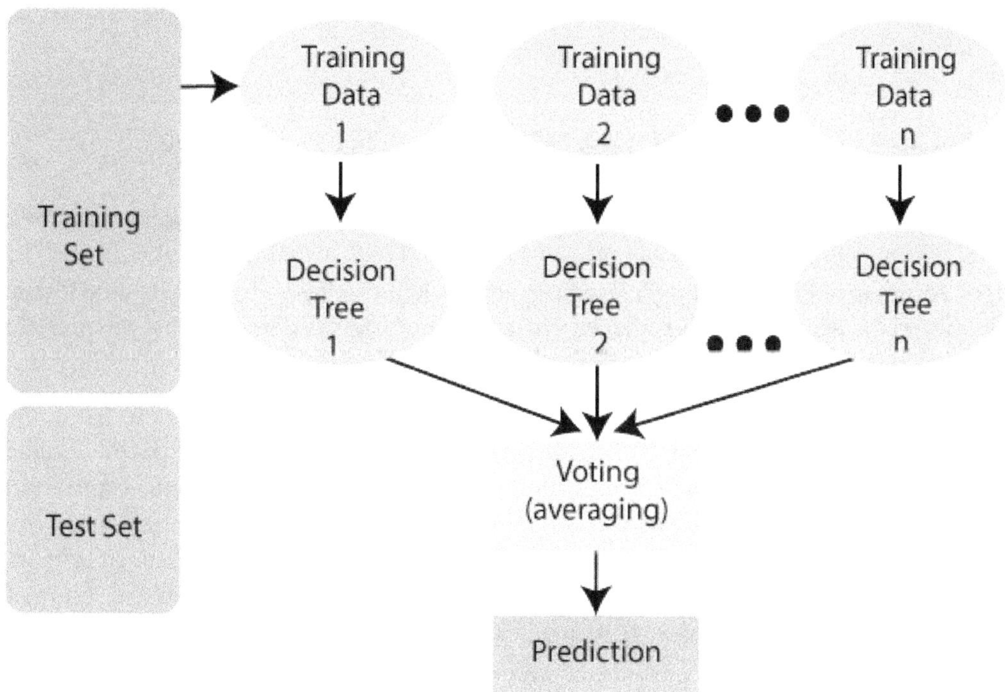

Fig 6.1 Random Forest Overview

In terms of innovation, Random Forests have made significant contributions. They are used in a variety of industries, from healthcare for illness detection to finance for risk assessment. Random Forests are robust because they can handle huge datasets with increased dimensionality. They can handle missing numbers and maintain accuracy even when a significant amount of the data is missing. One of the most significant contributions is their capacity to offer feature importances, which can be used for feature selection in a machine learning project. This is very useful when working with data sets with a high number of attributes and need to select the most important ones.

The Random Forest technique is versatile and may be used for both classification and regression issues, resulting in excellent accuracy in most circumstances. It performs well with noisy data and is less sensitive to outliers, making it an excellent solution for a wide range of challenging issues in practice. Its capacity to run in parallel makes it very scalable, and it can be computed in a distributed environment. All of these characteristics make Random Forests a very adaptable and versatile algorithm, a breakthrough that has expanded the scope and applications of machine learning.

In terms of implementation, Rust has several libraries that enable Random Forests, including 'RustLearn' and 'RustML'. These libraries contain pre-written structures and methods that make Random Forest models easier to implement, allowing you to benefit from Rust's speed and safety while developing complicated machine learning models. As we move through this chapter, we will learn more about how to implement Random Forests, including the entire range of its capabilities and fine-tuning choices.

Random Forest Classifier Architecture

The architecture of a Random Forest classifier is a fascinating blend of simplicity and complexity. At its core, a Random Forest is a collection of Decision Trees, usually trained with the "bagging" method, or sometimes even "pasting". Bagging allows each tree to be trained on a different subset of the training data, sampled with replacement from the original dataset. This ensures that each tree is learning from a unique set of data points, reducing the risk of overfitting while maintaining the model's ability to generalize well to new data.

One essential aspect to delve into is "Feature Bagging", or Random Subspaces. Unlike single decision trees, where all features are considered for splitting at each node, Random Forests randomly select a subset of features for each split. This randomized feature selection introduces further diversity among the trees in the forest, making the ensemble less likely to overfit and more robust to noise in the data. This randomness in feature selection can be controlled by hyperparameters, often named `max_features`, which define the number of features to consider for making the best split.

Another intriguing aspect of Random Forests is "Out-of-Bag Evaluation". Since bagging involves sampling with replacement, some instances may be sampled multiple times for one model, while others may not be sampled at all. The instances that are not sampled are termed "out-of-bag" instances. These can be used as a validation set to evaluate the model's performance, thereby eliminating the need for a separate validation set. This makes the Random Forest algorithm efficient in terms of data utilization, and the Out-of-Bag (OOB) score provides an unbiased estimate of the model's generalization error.

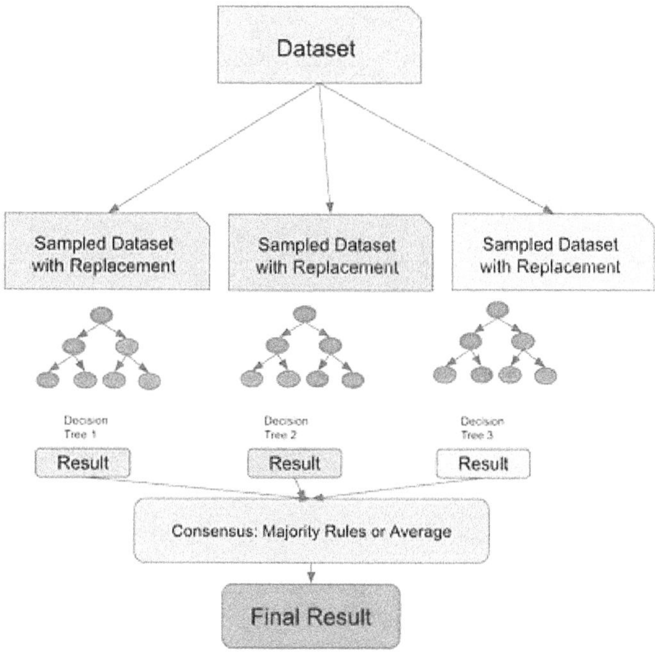

Fig 6.2 Working of Random Forest Classifier

A Random Forest is also capable of "Handling Imbalanced Classes". In a classification problem, it is common to encounter datasets where some classes have much fewer instances than others. Random Forests can be tuned to handle this imbalance effectively by adjusting class weights or through resampling techniques. This is crucial in scenarios like fraud detection or rare disease diagnosis, where the minority class is often more critical.

We learned about "Parallelization and Scalability". Random Forests inherently support parallelism. Each tree in the forest is independent of the others, which means multiple trees can be trained simultaneously. This feature makes Random Forests highly scalable and well-suited for big data applications. With Rust's concurrent computing capabilities, implementing a parallelized Random Forest can be highly efficient, making the algorithm even more appealing for practical applications.

Overall, the architecture of a Random Forest classifier is a masterpiece of ensemble learning, bringing together multiple elements like bagging, feature randomness, out-of-bag evaluation, and parallel computing.

Building Random Forest Model

Up and Running with RustLearn

RustLearn is a machine learning library that is designed for both performance and ease of use. It comes with a variety of tools for building and working with machine learning models, including Random Forests. One of the advantages of using RustLearn is that it provides a simple yet powerful interface for building models, without sacrificing the low-level control that Rust offers. This makes it a go-to choice for those who want to build robust and highly efficient machine learning models. It supports various algorithms and utilities for pre-processing, model evaluation, and hyperparameter tuning, among others.

Now, before diving into building the model, we need to include RustLearn in our project's Cargo.toml file. It can be added under dependencies like so:

```
[dependencies]

rustlearn = "0.5"
```

Once added, run cargo build to fetch the library and its dependencies.

Defining Random Forest Model

RustLearn's API for Random Forest is quite straightforward. You create a new instance of a Random Forest model by calling the RandomForest::new() method. This method takes several optional parameters, like the number of trees in the forest (num_trees) and the maximum depth for each tree (max_depth), among others. These hyperparameters can be adjusted to fine-tune the model's performance. For instance,

```
use rustlearn::ensemble::random_forest::Hyperparameters;

let num_trees = 100;

let max_depth = 10;

let model = Hyperparameters::new(num_trees).depth(max_depth);
```

Training and Predict Model

Once the model is defined, you can train it using the fit method. It takes the feature matrix X and the target vector y as arguments. Assume that X_train and y_train are your pre-processed training data.

```
model.fit(&X_train, &y_train).unwrap();
```

The **fit** method will construct the Random Forest based on the training data, taking into account the hyperparameters you've set. After training, you can make predictions using the **predict** method. Assume **X_test** is the feature matrix for the test set.

```
let prediction = model.predict(&X_test).unwrap();
```

The method returns a prediction vector that you can then compare with the actual labels to evaluate the model's performance.

RustLearn's Model Evaluation

RustLearn also provides utilities for model evaluation like confusion matrices, accuracy, and other metrics. However, you can also use the prediction output to manually compute these metrics. Considering we've already covered model evaluation techniques in the previous decision tree chapter, we will assume you can apply those methods here as well on your own.

The combination of Rust's performance features with RustLearn creates a powerful and efficient method for handling machine learning problems. Always keep in mind that fully grasping Random Forests requires not just familiarity with the algorithm but also with the nuances of the programming language and library you're using. You will discover that RustLearn is an effective weapon in your machine learning arsenal as you get experience with it.

Comparison with Decision Tree Model

A Random Forest model against a Decision Tree model is like comparing the collective wisdom of a team to that of an individual's judgment. We look at the practical aspects of comparing a Random Forest model to a Decision Tree model using the Rust programming language. Using what you've learnt in earlier chapters, we'll import and preprocess the dataset using RustLearn.

Creating Respective Models

You would initiate a Decision Tree model in RustLearn like so:

```
use rustlearn::trees::decision_tree::Hyperparameters;

let max_depth = 10;
```

```
let criterion = "entropy";

let dt_model = Hyperparameters::new(max_depth).criterion(criterion);
```

Train it using the **fit** method with your training data:

```
dt_model.fit(&X_train, &y_train).unwrap();
```

Similarly, for Random Forest, you would create a model like this:

```
use rustlearn::ensemble::random_forest::Hyperparameters;

let num_trees = 100;

let rf_model = Hyperparameters::new(num_trees).depth(max_depth);
```

And train it:

```
rf_model.fit(&X_train, &y_train).unwrap();
```

Evaluating Models

Both models can be evaluated using metrics like accuracy, precision, and recall. Assume you've used RustLearn's metrics or manually calculated these metrics for both models. You would typically find the Random Forest model to have better metrics due to its ensemble nature.

In code, after predictions, it might look something like this:

```
let dt_prediction = dt_model.predict(&X_test).unwrap();

let rf_prediction = rf_model.predict(&X_test).unwrap();

// Compute metrics for both and compare
```

Model Interpretability

Although Random Forest models generally provide a better generalization, they lack the interpretability that Decision Trees offer. A Decision Tree's decisions can be visualized and easily understood, which is not the case with Random Forests. This is an important aspect to consider, especially if you need to explain the model's decisions.

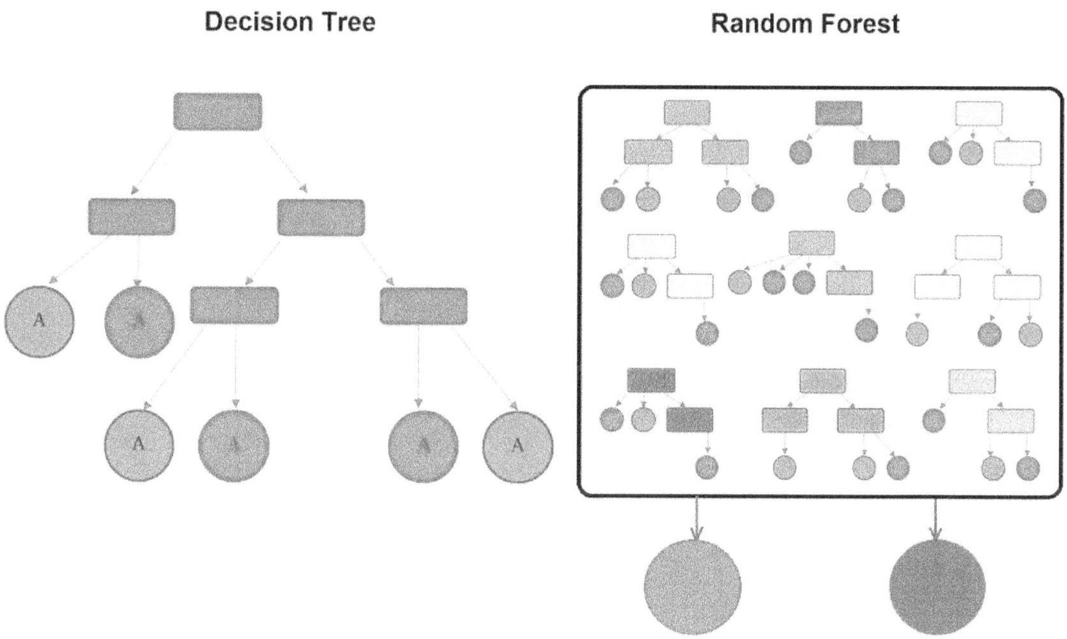

Fig 6.3 Decision Tree vs. Random Forest

Computational Cost

The computational cost is also worth noting. While a Decision Tree is generally faster to train, Random Forests, especially with a large number of trees, can be computationally expensive. However, they offer the advantage of parallelization, which Rust can handle efficiently.

Overfitting

If your Decision Tree model shows signs of overfitting, the Random Forest model will generally be more resilient to this due to its ensemble nature. You can easily compare this by looking at the performance metrics on both the training and test datasets for both models.

Feature Importance

Lastly, while both models provide insights into feature importance, Random Forests offer a more averaged and reliable measure due to their ensemble nature. This can be crucial for understanding which features are contributing most to the model's decisions.

Tuning Random Forests Hyperparameters

In the context of Random Forests, the hyperparameters you will often tune include the number of trees (n_estimators), maximum depth of each tree (max_depth), minimum samples required to split an internal node (min_samples_split), and others. You will generally perform this tuning manually, as RustLearn and many other Rust-based machine learning libraries don't provide in-built tools for hyperparameter search like GridSearchCV or RandomizedSearchCV available in Python's scikit-learn.

Manual Grid Search

The most straightforward way to perform hyperparameter tuning is by employing nested loops to iterate through different combinations of hyperparameters. After training the model with each combination, you evaluate it using a validation set or cross-validation. The set of hyperparameters that yield the best performance metric (e.g., accuracy, F1 score, etc.) are considered the optimal set.

```
let mut best_accuracy = 0.0;

let mut best_params = (0, 0);

for n_trees in [50, 100, 150].iter() {

 for max_depth in [10, 20, 30].iter() {

 let model = Hyperparameters::new(*n_trees).depth(*max_depth);

 model.fit(&X_train, &y_train).unwrap();

 let predictions = model.predict(&X_test).unwrap();

 let accuracy = compute_accuracy(&predictions, &y_test); // Assume a function to
compute accuracy

 if accuracy > best_accuracy {

 best_accuracy = accuracy;

 best_params = (*n_trees, *max_depth);

 }
```

```
}

}
```

Randomized Search

Another approach is to perform a randomized search where you randomly sample hyperparameters from a given range or distribution. This method is computationally less expensive than a grid search but can be equally effective in finding a good set of hyperparameters.

```
use rand::Rng;

let mut rng = rand::thread_rng();

let mut best_accuracy = 0.0;

let mut best_params = (0, 0);

for _ in 0..50 {

 let n_trees: usize = rng.gen_range(50..150);

 let max_depth: usize = rng.gen_range(10..30);

 let model = Hyperparameters::new(n_trees).depth(max_depth);

 model.fit(&X_train, &y_train).unwrap();

 let predictions = model.predict(&X_test).unwrap();

 let accuracy = compute_accuracy(&predictions, &y_test); // Assume a function to
compute accuracy

 if accuracy > best_accuracy {

 best_accuracy = accuracy;

 best_params = (n_trees, max_depth);

 }
```

}

Cross-Validation

To ensure that your hyperparameter tuning is robust and not biased towards a specific train-test split, you could employ k-fold cross-validation. This involves splitting your data into 'k' subsets (or folds), training your model 'k' times (each time leaving one of the k subsets out of training and using it as the test set), and then averaging the performance across all 'k' runs. RustLearn provides a `CrossValidation` trait that can be used for this purpose.

You may effectively tune the hyperparameters of a Random Forest model if you use any of the methods described above. The goal is to identify the ideal set that enhances the model's performance on previously unseen data, making it more generalizable and robust. Keep in mind that improving a model's performance relies heavily on hyperparameter tuning, which is a tedious and iterative process.

Errors and Troubleshooting

When implementing Random Forest models, several types of errors and challenges may arise, each requiring its unique approach for resolution.

#1 Overfitting

While Random Forests are generally resistant to overfitting, they're not entirely immune, especially when dealing with high-dimensional data.

Solution

Adjust the hyperparameters like `max_depth` to limit the depth of the trees or increase `min_samples_split` to require more samples for a split. Regularization techniques can also be employed. You can adjust these when you instantiate your Random Forest model:

```
let model =
Hyperparameters::new(n_trees).depth(max_depth).min_samples_split(min_samples);
```

#2 Memory Exhaustion

Random Forest models can be memory-intensive, especially with a large number of trees and deep trees.

Solution

You can look for opportunities to clear memory manually or optimize your data structures. If we are using the Vec datatype excessively, consider using slices or iterators. Using a 64-bit version of Rust can also help.

#3 Imbalanced Data

If your dataset is imbalanced, the model may be biased towards the majority class.

Solution

You can oversample the minority class or undersample the majority class to balance the dataset. Libraries like imbalanced-learn-rs can be useful for this. Alternatively, focus on metrics that are sensitive to class imbalance like F1-score, Precision, and Recall.

#4 High Dimensionality

If the dataset has too many features, it may slow down the model training process and make the model complex.

Solution

Feature selection can be performed to reduce dimensionality. Random Forest itself can be used for feature importance evaluation. The most important features can be retained, and the less important ones can be dropped.

#5 Parallelization Errors

When parallelizing the Random Forest algorithm, you might encounter errors related to data sharing and thread safety.

Solution

Rust's ownership model helps to some extent, but you should also use thread-safe data structures provided in the standard library or crates like crossbeam and rayon to ensure safety.

#6 Numerical Instabilities

Sometimes, numerical issues like underflow and overflow can cause problems.

Solution

Libraries like ndarray and nalgebra offer numerical stability for operations. Do not forget we are using these libraries' functionalities wherever possible. Also, scaling the features to a certain range can prevent these issues to an extent.

#7 Non-Numerical Data

Random Forest algorithms require numerical input, and hence categorical and textual data can pose a problem.

Solution

One-hot encoding or label encoding can be used to convert categorical variables into a format that could be provided to machine learning algorithms. For text data, techniques like TF-IDF or word embeddings can be used.

#8 Incomplete or Missing Data

Although we've covered data preprocessing, incomplete data can still be an issue.

Solution

Advanced techniques like data imputation can be applied to fill the missing values. Libraries for data imputation are limited but you can manually code to replace missing values with the mean or median.

#9 Incorrect Evaluation Metrics

Using the wrong evaluation metric can lead to incorrect conclusions about the model's performance.

Solution

Always align the evaluation metric with the business objective. If you are dealing with imbalanced classes, metrics like accuracy may not be suitable. Opt for precision, recall, or the F1-score instead.

Problems that develop during the implementation of Random Forest models can be better handled if you are familiar with these possible hazards and how to avoid them. Each issue has a unique remedy, and the key is to precisely diagnose the problem in order to apply the most effective solution.

Summary

In this chapter, we looked at Random Forests, an ensemble learning technique that provides a more robust and accurate alternative to individual decision trees. We investigated the design and internal workings of Random Forest classifiers, learning how they combine predictions from many decision trees to produce more accurate and stable predictions. We also explored how to build a Random Forest model using the RustLearn library. The chapter discussed how ensemble approaches such as Random Forests contribute to machine learning innovation by improving predictive performance and providing novel characteristics such as feature significance.

Hyperparameter tuning was an important aspect of our research, as we learnt how to manually modify parameters such as the number of trees (n_estimators) and maximum depth (max_depth), among others. We also learned about alternative methods for validating the model's performance, such as manual grid search and randomized search, and how to implement them. The need of selecting the appropriate performance metric was underlined, as was the need to connect it with the project's goal.

We addressed a variety of issues and faults that could arise during the implementation phase, including overfitting, memory depletion, and dealing with imbalanced data. Each of these issues was addressed with realistic solutions, ranging from hyperparameter tweaks and data resampling approaches to the use of specific Rust libraries and features for optimization. The chapter provided you with the skills and information necessary to detect and remedy these difficulties, resulting in more effective and robust Random Forest models.

We used real examples to compare Random Forests to single decision trees, highlighting the benefits of employing the former for more complicated issues. The chapter also covered feature extraction, emphasizing how Random Forests might be utilized for feature selection due to their capacity to calculate feature importance. Overall, the chapter provided a thorough, hands-on approach to understanding and implementing Random Forest classifiers, laying the groundwork for tackling more sophisticated machine learning models and techniques.

Chapter 7: Support Vector Machines In Action

Introduction to Support Vector Machines

Support Vector Machines (SVM) are a type of supervised learning algorithms that are generally used for classification, but can also be used for regression. SVM, which originated with the idea of determining the hyperplane that best divides a dataset into classes, has played an important role in a variety of disciplines, including image recognition, text classification, and bioinformatics. One of SVM's distinguishing properties is its capacity to operate in infinite dimensional spaces, courtesy to the "kernel trick," which allows it to translate input data into higher-dimensional areas indirectly. This is especially beneficial when working with data that is not linearly separable in its native space.

In NLP, SVM is often used for text categorization problems. Because of the high dimensionality of text data, SVM is a great choice for handling a variety of features. For example, in sentiment analysis, when the goal is to categorize sentiments as good, negative, or neutral, SVM can perform admirably. In bioinformatics, SVM algorithms are also used to classify proteins and cancers. They can handle the high-dimensional and sparse data that is frequent in these domains.

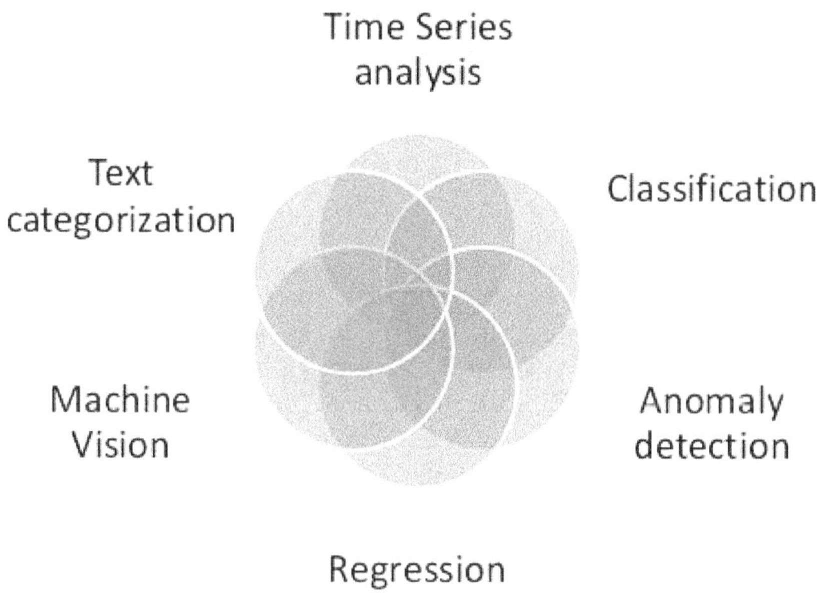

Fig 7.1 Applications of SVM

SVM is very useful in the financial sector, particularly for predicting stock market price movements. SVM may be trained to forecast whether a stock price will rise or fall based on previous data, allowing investors to make more informed decisions. SVM is also used in healthcare to forecast and classify diseases. Medical experts utilize SVM models to forecast diseases such as diabetes or cancer based on symptoms and test findings, saving valuable time and resources in the process.

However, SVM is not without its drawbacks. When the data is not linearly separable, one of the most important difficulties is determining the appropriate kernel function. The intricacy of selecting the appropriate kernel function can be intimidating for newcomers. Additionally, SVMs are susceptible to noise. A few mislabeled instances can have a significant impact on performance. Furthermore, with huge datasets, processing complexity can be an impediment. Despite these obstacles, SVM's adaptability and durability in handling high-dimensional data make it one of the preferred algorithms among machine learning practitioners.

SVMs have numerous uses in image identification problems. For example, in handwritten digit identification, where each image can be viewed as a point in a high-dimensional space, SVM can identify the hyperplane that separates these points depending on their respective classes. The same principle applies to facial recognition technology, in which SVMs can be trained to accurately detect faces.

To summarize, Support Vector Machines provide a robust and versatile solution for solving both linear and nonlinear problems in a variety of domains. Their capacity to handle high-dimensional data successfully makes them invaluable in modern machine learning applications, notwithstanding the difficulties associated with their implementation.

Types of Support Vector Machines

SVMs are classified into two types: linear SVMs and kernel SVMs. In this section, we will delve into the complexities of each kind, beginning with the Linear Support Vector Machine.

Linear SVM

In Linear SVM, the objective is to find a hyperplane that distinctly classifies data points into separate classes. In a two-dimensional space, this hyperplane is a line. However, in higher dimensions, it becomes a hyperplane, essentially serving as a 'boundary' that maximizes the margin between different classes. The margin is defined as the distance between the closest points (also known as support vectors) of different classes to the hyperplane. Mathematically, this is achieved by solving an optimization problem that maximizes this margin, subject to the constraint that the points must be classified correctly.

The equation of the hyperplane is given by,

$w \cdot x + b = 0$, where w is the weight vector, and b is the bias.

Architecture of Linear SVM

The architecture of a Linear SVM is relatively straightforward. It comprises the input space, the feature space (which, in this case, is the same as the input space), the hyperplane, and the margin. The algorithm tries to find the optimal hyperplane by solving a convex optimization problem. Linear SVMs are often implemented using optimization techniques like Quadratic Programming or gradient descent. Once the hyperplane parameters w and b are optimized, the model can make predictions for new data points by simply substituting them into the hyperplane equation.

Kernel SVM

Kernel SVM is used when the data cannot be separated linearly. In such circumstances, the data is transformed into a higher-dimensional space, where it is linearly separable. This mapping is carried out utilizing a function known as the 'kernel function'. The Polynomial Kernel, Radial Basis Function (RBF) Kernel, and Sigmoid Kernel are the three most widely utilized kernel functions. The purpose of employing a kernel is to compute the dot product of converted vectors in a higher-dimensional space without having to conduct the transformation. This is known as the 'kernel trick', because it enables SVM to operate well in infinite-dimensional spaces.

Architecture of Kernel SVM

The architecture of Kernel SVM is more complex due to the involvement of the kernel function. The input space is first transformed into a feature space using this function. The feature space can be of much higher dimensionality than the input space. The hyperplane is then found in this new feature space. The kernel function is central to this architecture, and choosing the right one is crucial for the performance of the SVM. The kernel function effectively replaces the dot product in the feature space, allowing for the application of linear methods (like finding a hyperplane) in a transformed version of the problem.

Differences and Commonality

While the goal of both support vector machines (SVMs) is to optimize the margin between classes, the spaces in which they locate the hyperplane are different. In contrast to Linear SVM, which uses the original feature space, Kernel SVM uses a changed feature space. Another distinction is computational complexity; Linear SVM is often faster and requires less computer power than Kernel SVM, particularly on large datasets.

SVM Modeling: Data Load, Preprocess and Model Build

Coronavirus Tweets Dataset

To gain practical expertise with SVM Modeling, we will work with the Coronavirus Twitter tweets dataset, which captures public mood during the pandemic. The dataset contains Twitter tweets from 44,955 individuals expressing their sentiments about the Coronavirus pandemic.

The file can be downloaded from the following Github repository:

https://github.com/kittenpub/database-repository/blob/main/Corona_NLP_train.csv

The dataset comprises multiple dimensions of information including 'TweetAt' (date of the tweet), 'UserName', 'ScreenName', 'Location', 'TweetText', and 'Sentiment'. For our machine learning model, the most relevant features are 'TweetText' and 'Sentiment'. The 'TweetText' serves as the feature set *X*, and 'Sentiment' serves as the label set *y*. The 'Sentiment' field have categories like 'Positive', 'Neutral', and 'Negative', which the SVM model will aim to predict based on the 'TweetText'.

Loading Data with CSV Crate

Rust's **csv** library provides robust functionality for reading CSV files. We can use the **ReaderBuilder** to create a **Reader** struct, which allows us to read each row of the dataset.

Given below is a snippet of how to read the relevant columns:

```
use csv::ReaderBuilder;

use std::error::Error;

fn read_csv() -> Result<(), Box<dyn Error>> {

 let mut reader = ReaderBuilder::new().from_path("/path/to/Corona_NLP_train.csv")?;

 let mut tweet_texts = Vec::new();

 let mut sentiments = Vec::new();

 for result in reader.deserialize() {

 let record: TweetRecord = result?;

 tweet_texts.push(record.TweetText);

 sentiments.push(record.Sentiment);

 }

 Ok(())

}

#[derive(Debug, Deserialize)]
```

```
struct TweetRecord {
 TweetText: String,
 Sentiment: String,
}
```

Using Rust's String Methods

Once we have the 'TweetText' and 'Sentiment' in vectors, the next step is preprocessing. Text data needs to be cleaned and transformed into a format that is usable by the SVM model. Cleaning often involves converting text to lowercase, removing punctuations, and stemming words. The Rust standard library provides a range of String methods for such operations.

Given below is a simple example to clean a single tweet:

```
fn clean_text(tweet: &str) -> String {
 tweet.to_lowercase()
 .chars()
 .filter(|&c| c.is_alphabetic() || c.is_whitespace())
 .collect::<String>()
}
```

Using Bag-of-Words or TF-IDF

After cleaning, you need to convert the textual data into numerical form, usually through a technique like Bag-of-Words (BoW) or Term Frequency-Inverse Document Frequency (TF-IDF). You can accomplish this by writing a function that maps unique words to integers and then transforms each tweet into a vector of these integers. Libraries like rust-tfidf can help with more advanced transformations.

SVM Model Building

Finally, for model building, you can use the RustLearn library, which offers a variety of machine learning algorithms, including SVM. The library allows you to specify the type of kernel, regularization constant, and other hyperparameters:

```
use rustlearn::prelude::*;

use rustlearn::svm::SVM;

fn main() {

 let model = SVM::new(Linear::default(), Hyperparameters::default());

 // Assume X_train and y_train are your preprocessed training data and labels

 model.fit(&X_train, &y_train).unwrap();

}
```

By the end of these steps, you will have a functioning SVM model built with Rust, trained on the dataset of Twitter sentiments about the Coronavirus pandemic. This model can then be used for making predictions or for further analysis, which are topics you mentioned you can like to explore in subsequent sections.

Perform Training and Predictions

Once you've preprocessed your data and transformed it into a numerical form, the next steps are to train the model and use it to make predictions as below.

Splitting Data into Training and Test Sets

A good rule of thumb is to create separate sets of data for training and testing before beginning training. That way, you may test how well the model does on data that it has never seen before. One option is to manually slice the arrays, but another is to use a machine learning library in Rust that offers this feature.

```
// Assume data is your features and target is your labels

let (X_train, X_test, y_train, y_test) = train_test_split(&data, &target, 0.2);
```

Training the SVM Model

After splitting the data, proceed to train the SVM model using the `fit` method. This method takes in your training features and labels and adjusts the model parameters accordingly.

```
use rustlearn::prelude::*;

use rustlearn::svm::SVM;

fn main() {

 let model = SVM::new(Linear::default(), Hyperparameters::default());

 model.fit(&X_train, &y_train).unwrap();

}
```

Making Predictions

Once the model is trained, you use it to make predictions on new or unseen data. The **predict** method in RustLearn's SVM implementation can be used for this purpose. This method takes in a feature matrix and returns a vector of predictions.

```
let predictions = model.predict(&X_test).unwrap();
```

Assessing Model Accuracy

Once the predictions have been acquired, it is usual to evaluate the performance of the model by comparing them to the actual labels. The F1-score, recall, accuracy, and precision are among the most popular measures as discussed in the previous chapter. Although not all of these metrics have built-in methods in RustLearn, they can be easily implemented in the next section.

```
let accuracy = y_test.iter()

 .zip(predictions.iter())

 .filter(|&(true_label, predicted)| true_label == predicted)

 .count() as f64 / y_test.len() as f64;
```

In this way, we are able to train the SVM model and use it for prediction, while also evaluating its performance using various metrics.

Predictions Evaluation and Hyperparameter

Tuning

After you've obtained predictions from the trained model, the next step is to evaluate these predictions against the actual labels to gauge the model's effectiveness. Evaluation metrics like accuracy, precision, recall, and F1-score can help assess performance.

Calculating Accuracy

Accuracy is one of the simplest metrics to understand. It's the ratio of the number of correct predictions to the total number of predictions.

```
let accuracy = y_test.iter()
 .zip(predictions.iter())
 .filter(|&(true_label, predicted)| true_label == predicted)
 .count() as f64 / y_test.len() as f64;
```

Calculating Precision and Recall

Precision and recall are more nuanced metrics that are particularly useful when the classes are imbalanced. Precision measures the accuracy of the positive predictions, while recall measures the model's ability to identify all the positive cases.

```
let (mut true_positives, mut false_positives, mut false_negatives) = (0, 0, 0);
for (true_label, predicted) in y_test.iter().zip(predictions.iter()) {
 if *true_label == 1 && *predicted == 1 {
 true_positives += 1;
 } else if *true_label == 0 && *predicted == 1 {
 false_positives += 1;
 } else if *true_label == 1 && *predicted == 0 {
 false_negatives += 1;
```

```
}

}

let precision = true_positives as f64 / (true_positives + false_positives) as f64;

let recall = true_positives as f64 / (true_positives + false_negatives) as f64;
```

After evaluating the model, the next step is tuning the hyperparameters to improve its performance. Hyperparameter tuning is often performed through techniques like grid search or random search. For SVM, the hyperparameters that are commonly tuned include the regularization term (C), the kernel type, and, in the case of RBF kernel, the gamma value.

Grid Search in Rust

You could perform grid search manually by looping through the possible combinations of hyperparameters. For each combination, you would train a model, evaluate it using a validation set, and store the performance metrics. At the end, you choose the hyperparameters that gave the best performance.

```
let c_values = vec![0.1, 1.0, 10.0];

let kernel_types = vec!["linear", "rbf"];

let mut best_accuracy = 0.0;

let mut best_params = ("", 0.0);

for c in &c_values {

 for kernel in &kernel_types {

 let model = SVM::new(KernelType::from(*kernel), Hyperparameters::new(*c));

 model.fit(&X_train, &y_train).unwrap();

 let predictions = model.predict(&X_validation).unwrap();

 let accuracy = calculate_accuracy(&y_validation, &predictions); // Assume this
function is implemented
```

```
if accuracy > best_accuracy {

best_accuracy = accuracy;

best_params = (*kernel, *c);

}

}

}
```

This approach is naive but effective for a reasonable range of hyperparameter values. More advanced techniques like random search or Bayesian optimization can also be implemented, but they would require more extensive setup.

Dataset and Model Update

Data in quickly changing environments, such as social media sentiment (in your instance, Twitter tweets concerning the coronavirus), is rarely stationary. It evolves with time, so a model trained today may not be as useful in a month or even a week. Updating the model to reflect new data is critical to maintaining its effectiveness. In this section, we will go over some methods for updating your SVM model in response to changes in your dataset.

Incremental Learning

The first concept to understand is incremental learning, where the model learns continuously as new data comes in. Some algorithms naturally support incremental learning; however, SVMs typically require retraining from scratch with the combined old and new data. Therefore, when you get an updated dataset, you can usually concatenate it with the old dataset and retrain the model.

```
// Assume `old_data` and `new_data` are the old and new datasets, respectively

let combined_data = concatenate_datasets(old_data, new_data); // Assume this function is implemented

let model = train_svm(combined_data); // Assume `train_svm` trains the SVM and returns the model
```

Data Retention Policies

Retraining the model with all the historical data may not be feasible or necessary. Sometimes, old data becomes irrelevant, and retaining all of it can even degrade the model's performance. One approach is to set a data retention policy, where you only keep the last 'N' records or the data for the last 'M' days. This policy helps in reducing the computational burden and possibly improving the model's relevance.

```
// Assume `retain_latest_data` retains only the latest 'N' records

let reduced_data = retain_latest_data(combined_data); // Assume this function is
implemented

let model = train_svm(reduced_data);
```

Versioning Models

It's good practice to version your models when you update them. Versioning helps in keeping track of performance changes over time and aids in debugging. When a new model is trained, it is saved with a unique identifier, often timestamped. This way, you can always roll back to an earlier version if needed.

```
// Saving the model with a timestamp

let timestamp = get_current_timestamp(); // Assume this function is implemented

save_model(&model, format!("SVM_Model_{}", timestamp)); // Assume this function
saves the model
```

Automating Updates

To make the update process more efficient, you can automate it using Rust's task scheduling libraries or external tools like cron jobs. You can schedule a script to pull the latest data, preprocess it, retrain the model, and update the version automatically. This automation ensures that your model is always up-to-date without manual intervention.

```
// Pseudo-code for an automated update script

fn update_model() {
```

```
let new_data = fetch_new_data(); // Assume this function fetches the new data

let combined_data = concatenate_datasets(load_old_data(), new_data); // Load old data and concatenate

let model = train_svm(retain_latest_data(combined_data));

save_model(&model, format!("SVM_Model_{}", get_current_timestamp()));

}
```

If you use these methods, your SVM model will continue to work well regardless of changes to the underlying data. This method of upgrading models is a continuous activity that occurs throughout the lifecycle of a machine learning project.

Model Rollbacks

A crucial feature that strengthens and guarantees your machine learning pipeline is the option to revert to an earlier version of the model. There are a lot of situations where going back to an earlier state would be helpful, such as when a new model version isn't working as planned or when it brings strange behaviors. The following explains how to add rewind capabilities in a Rust-based machine learning system.

Model Versioning System

The first step in facilitating a rollback is to implement a structured model versioning system. As previously stated, each time you train and save a new model, it should be assigned a unique identification. This identification could be a date or a semantic version number, such as "Model_v1.2."

```
// Pseudo code to demonstrate model saving with a version

let version = "Model_v1.2";

save_model(&model, version);
```

Metadata Storage

Alongside the model, it is good to save metadata that describes the model. The metadata could include things like the date of training, the dataset used, performance metrics, and so on. You can use Rust's file handling libraries to create a metadata file alongside each model version.

```
// Pseudo code to save metadata

let metadata = create_metadata(&model); // Assume this function creates metadata

save_metadata(&metadata, version);
```

Version Catalog

Keep a catalog or a log file that lists all the versions of the models available, perhaps in a simple CSV or JSON file. This catalog allows you to quickly inspect which versions are available for rollback.

```
// Pseudo code to update a version catalog

update_version_catalog(version, &metadata);
```

Rollback and Testing

The rollback itself is a straightforward procedure. You would simply load the older model version into your application. However, ensure that when you do this, you also revert any data transformations or feature engineering steps to be compatible with the older model version.

```
// Pseudo code for rollback

let version_to_rollback = "Model_v1.1";

let model = load_model(version_to_rollback);
```

Once the rollback is complete, it is crucial to test the model to ensure it is performing as expected. Run the model on a test dataset and compare the metrics to those recorded in the metadata. This step ensures that the rollback was successful and that the model is functioning correctly.

```
// Pseudo code to test model after rollback

let test_data = load_test_data(); // Assume this function loads a test dataset

let metrics = evaluate_model(&model, &test_data);
```

Lastly, document the rollback. Make an entry in the version catalog or another log file indicating the rollback, the reason for it, and any observed changes in performance. This documentation helps in auditing and future debugging.

```
// Pseudo code to document rollback

document_rollback(version_to_rollback, reason, &metrics);
```

If you follow these steps, your machine learning pipeline will be very reliable in a production setting and able to withstand changes better.

Summary

One of the most effective machine learning classification methods, Support Vector Machines were thoroughly explored in this chapter. We began by studying the core principles of SVM, particularly its unique methodology for determining the best hyperplane for classifying data points. We looked at Linear SVM and Non-Linear SVM, the two most common kinds of support vector machines (SVMs), and how their architectures and input formats differ. The chapter also discussed SVM's adaptability in addressing complicated issues such as text classification and picture recognition, underlining its importance in the machine learning environment.

We next applied SVM to a real and true dataset of Twitter tweets about the coronavirus pandemic. This hands-on section explained the entire model-building process, from data loading to feature engineering. We also learnt how data preparation improves model performance. Each step was meticulously presented to ensure a thorough understanding of the technical aspects of developing an SVM model with Rust.

The final half of the chapter focused on model evaluation, hyperparameter tuning, and metric comprehension. We learnt how to successfully tweak the hyperparameters of our SVM model and evaluate its performance using measures such as accuracy, precision, and F1-score. The chapter also discussed how to compare SVM output to other machine learning models, giving a detailed overview of its benefits and drawbacks. Finally, we discussed key techniques for maintaining and updating SVM models, including as rollback procedures.

Chapter 8: Simplifying Naive Bayes and k-NN

Naive Bayes and k-NN Overview

In previous chapters, we looked at a variety of machine learning algorithms, each with its own set of strengths, limits, and applications. We began by studying the fundamentals of linear and logistic regression, trying to grasp how these algorithms fit into the supervised learning environment. We then explored decision trees and random forests, as well as ensemble methods that boost performance by building on simpler models. SVM reached another milestone by providing a novel method to classification challenges. Each technique was tested practically, with hands-on examples based on real and true datasets, all within the Rust programming environment.

Coming up next, we'll take a look at two more machine learning algorithms that are both basic and powerful: k-Nearest Neighbours (k-NN) and Naive Bayes. The attractiveness of these strategies stems from their simplicity and ease of interpretation. Naive Bayes is based on Bayes' theorem and makes the 'naive' assumption that characteristics are independent. Despite its simplicity, it is very beneficial for text categorization tasks like spam filtering and sentiment analysis. Its probabilistic nature enables it to not only make predictions, but also evaluate their uncertainty.

In contrast, k-NN is a learning method that works with instances. It does not actively train a model; rather, it memorizes the training data. When a new data point comes, k-NN examines the 'k' nearest points in the training set and produces a prediction based on the majority class of those neighbors. This technique has a wide range of applications, including classification and regression. The main advantage of k-NN is its simplicity: there is no need for iterative training, and it is frequently easy to explain why the algorithm made a particular prediction.

Naive Bayes and k-NN are based on fundamental mathematical and statistical principles, making them simple to comprehend and apply. However, their simplicity does not detract from its utility. They are frequently employed in a variety of sectors, including healthcare and finance, and they make good introduction algorithms for individuals new to machine learning. Their interpretability and user-friendliness make them great options for basic models and rapid prototyping, particularly when dealing with a performance-and efficiency-focused language like Rust.

Naive Bayes Classifier Architecture

Naive Bayes is a classification technique that relies on Bayes' Theorem, a fundamental idea in probability theory and statistics. The theorem describes how to determine the probability of a hypothesis based on prior knowledge. In the case of Naive Bayes, the hypothesis is the anticipated label, and prior knowledge is the characteristics of the data point being classified.

The theorem's equation is as follows: $P(A|B) = [P(B|A) \times P(A)] / P(B)$, where A and B represent events. A is the event that a data point belongs to a specific class, whereas B is the event that we observed a specific feature vector. We are interested in the probability of a class given a feature vector, denoted as $P(A|B)$.

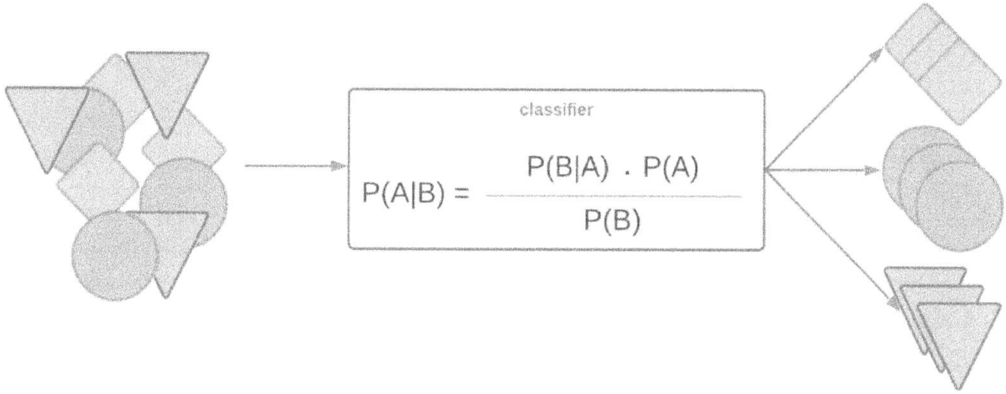

Fig 8.1 Naïve Bayes Classifier

The 'Naive' in Naive Bayes refers to the premise that all features are independent of one another, given the class name. While this assumption is rarely valid in practical applications, it simplifies calculations and frequently produces a model that performs admirably. In the equation, P(B|A) represents the likelihood, P(A) the prior probability of each class, and P(B) the evidence. These are the foundational elements of the Naive Bayes architecture. The likelihood P(B|A) indicates how well your features explain observed outcomes, or how likely it is that a data point belongs to a specific class. Because of the naïve independence assumption, naïve Bayes calculates this for each characteristic independently before multiplying them together. This significantly reduces the computational complexity. The prior P(A) represents the probability of each class in the absence of any additional information. It is frequently determined using the training data; for example, if 60% of your training samples are 'Positive' and 40% are 'Negative,' those percentages form your prior probability. In some circumstances, you may prefer to set these priors depending on domain expertise.

The Evidence P(B) is a normalizing constant that ensures all probability add to one. It is often determined by summing over all classes, taking into consideration both the prior and likelihood. However, because P(B) is constant for a given input, we generally ignore it during the model training phase, instead concentrate on optimizing P(B|A)×P(A).

To summarize, the naïve Bayes algorithm combines Bayes' Theorem with the naïve assumption of feature independence to produce a highly efficient and frequently shockingly accurate classifier. Each component, from likelihood to previous evidence, is critical to the algorithm's operation and allows it to generate probabilistic predictions regarding class membership. Despite its simplicity, it is an effective machine learning technique, especially when computational resources are constrained, as is often the case in Rust-based systems.

Building Naive Bayes Model

We dive into building a Naive Bayes classifier using the heart prediction dataset. We will use Rust and a relevant package like RustLearn to build the model. Assuming the data is already loaded and preprocessed, we focus on defining our features and labels. In most Rust ML packages, data is often represented in array-like structures. Do not forget your features (X) and labels (y) are separated and properly formatted.

The first step in building a Naive Bayes model is to initialize it. Depending on your package, this could be as simple as calling a NaiveBayes::new() function. This step typically involves specifying the type of Naive Bayes model you wish to use: Gaussian, Multinomial, or Bernoulli. Each type is best suited for a specific kind of data. For the heart prediction dataset, a Gaussian Naive Bayes could be a good choice given that the features are continuous.

```
use rustlearn::prelude::*;

use rustlearn::naive_bayes::{GaussianNB};

let mut model = GaussianNB::new();
```

Once the model is initialized, the next step is to fit it to your training data. The fit method usually takes in your features and labels and trains the model based on the Bayes theorem, calculating all the probabilities needed for prediction.

```
model.fit(&X_train, &y_train).unwrap();
```

After fitting, the model is ready to make predictions. You can use the predict method to get the predicted labels for your test set. It's also possible to get the probabilities for each class, which can be useful for understanding the model's confidence in its predictions.

```
let predictions = model.predict(&X_test).unwrap();
```

The beauty of Naive Bayes lies in its simplicity and efficiency. Despite making naive assumptions about feature independence, it often performs quite well in practice. It's especially useful for baseline models, giving you a quick and dirty classifier that you can use to compare more complex models against. And in a language like Rust, where efficiency is a key selling point, Naive Bayes adheres well to the philosophy of doing more with less.

To summarize, developing a Naive Bayes classifier entails initializing the model, fitting it to your data, producing predictions, and then assessing those predictions. Each of these processes is critical and helps to the efficiency of your machine learning pipeline. As a result of its computing efficiency and relative simplicity, Naive Bayes has become an algorithm of choice for efficient and rapid categorization.

Building k-NN Model

Moving on from Naive Bayes, we will look at the k-NN method, which is another simple yet successful machine learning technique. The underlying logic of this method differs from that of Naive Bayes. While Naive Bayes focuses on probabilities and statistical measures, k-NN harnesses the power of similarity metrics. The goal of k-NN is to classify an unknown point using the labels of its 'k' nearest points in the feature space. The 'k' in k-NN represents the number of nearest neighbors that the algorithm considers while making predictions. The simplicity of k-NN makes it an ideal tool for rapid prototyping and baseline modeling, and it is equally simple to implement.

We start by initializing the k-NN model. Depending on the Rust library we are using, this could look something like `KNN::new(k, distance_metric)`. The initialization usually requires you to specify the number of neighbors ('k') and the distance metric to use (Euclidean, Manhattan, etc.).

```
use rustlearn::neighbors::KNNClassifier;

let k = 3; // Number of neighbors

let model = KNNClassifier::new(k);
```

Once you have initialized your k-NN model, the next step, similar to Naive Bayes, is to fit it to your training data. k-NN doesn't really "train" in the way that other algorithms do; rather, it memorizes the training dataset. The `fit` function in this context will store the feature vectors and their corresponding labels so that they can be used for future similarity comparisons.

```
model.fit(&X_train, &y_train).unwrap();
```

After fitting, we are ready to make predictions. The `predict` function takes a dataset and returns a set of labels by evaluating the 'k' nearest training points for each instance in the dataset.

```
let predictions = model.predict(&X_test).unwrap();
```

The computational complexity of k-NN can be a downside, especially for large datasets. Each prediction requires a full scan of the training data to find the 'k' nearest points, which can be computationally expensive. However, various optimization techniques like KD-Trees can help, although such advanced features might not be readily available in all Rust libraries.

To evaluate your k-NN model, you can use the same metrics as you would with any other classification model: accuracy, F1 score, confusion matrix, etc. The evaluation step helps you understand how well your model generalizes to unseen data.

```
let accuracy = accuracy_score(&y_test, &predictions);
```

To sum up, k-NN offers a different paradigm for classification, relying on geometric distance metrics rather than probabilistic models. Its ease of use and straightforward implementation make it a valuable addition to your machine learning toolbox. While it may not be the most computationally efficient algorithm for large datasets, its simplicity and effectiveness often make it a useful first step in the exploratory phase of data science projects.

Naive Bayes and k-NN Model Comparison

Naive Bayes and k-NN may appear to be similar at a glance, as both are commonly used for classification tasks and are considered to be relatively simple to understand and implement. However, these two algorithms come from entirely different schools of thought within machine learning and offer distinct advantages and disadvantages. The comparison can be thought of as a juxtaposition between a probabilistic, assumption-driven model (Naive Bayes) and an instance-based, lazy-learning model (k-NN).

Starting with Naive Bayes, this algorithm is based on the application of Bayes' theorem, and it assumes that the features in the dataset are conditionally independent. This assumption, although naive (as the name suggests), often holds well enough in practice to make Naive Bayes a powerful tool for classification. Naive Bayes is particularly effective for high-dimensional datasets where features are mostly independent. It's also computationally efficient, as it doesn't require to store the entire dataset, but rather just the probabilities calculated during training. The algorithm works well with categorical data, and it is commonly used in text classification problems, such as spam filtering or sentiment analysis.

Contrast this with k-NN, which makes no assumptions about the underlying data distribution. k-NN doesn't require a training phase in the traditional sense; it memorized the entire dataset instead. This approach makes it more versatile in handling complex feature relationships that do not meet the independence assumptions of Naive Bayes. However, the trade-off is computational complexity during the prediction phase, especially for large datasets. k-NN is a non-parametric algorithm, meaning it makes decisions based on the entire dataset, without any underlying assumptions about the data's distribution. Because k-NN relies on a distance metric, it is also more sensitive to feature scaling, and preprocessing steps like normalization or standardization become crucial.

Another crucial difference lies in interpretability. Naive Bayes models are generally easier to understand because they provide probabilistic outputs that can be interpreted as the model's confidence in a particular classification. You can easily extract the conditional probabilities for each feature and understand how the model is making decisions. k-NN lacks this level of interpretability; while you can consider the 'k' closest neighbors for an insight into the decision-making process, the model does not offer an intuitive probabilistic explanation for its classifications.

When considering which model to implement, your decision will likely hinge on several factors, including the nature of your dataset, the computational resources at your disposal, and the level of interpretability you require. If we are dealing with a high-dimensional, text-based dataset and need a quick, efficient algorithm, Naive Bayes could be the way to go. If your dataset has complex, non-linear relationships and you have the computational resources to handle the heavier prediction phase, k-NN may be more appropriate. Both models have their places in a data scientist's toolkit, and the best choice often depends on the specific needs of the project at hand.

Errors and Troubleshooting

#1 Model not Converging

Your Naive Bayes or k-NN model may not converge during training, meaning that the model's performance doesn't improve or stabilize.

Solution

This could happen due to a variety of reasons—wrong selection of features, inappropriate hyperparameters, or even data quality. First, reevaluate the features we are using; maybe perform a feature importance analysis. Second, try different hyperparameters; k-NN is sensitive to the choice of 'k', and Naive Bayes has different variants that assume different distributions for the data. Finally, inspect your data; ensure it is normalized and doesn't contain outliers that could affect the learning process.

```
// For k-NN, try varying k

let knn_model = KNN::new(3); // instead of KNN::new(5)



// For Naive Bayes, try a different distribution assumption

let naive_bayes_model = NaiveBayes::new(Gaussian); // instead of
NaiveBayes::new(Multinomial);
```

#2 File not Found during Serialization/Deserialization

When you try to serialize or deserialize the model, the file path may be incorrect, causing a "File Not Found" error.

Solution

Ensure that the file path is correct and that you have read/write permissions for that directory. Use Rust's **Path** and **PathBuf** for more robust file path handling.

```
use std::path::Path;

if Path::new("naive_bayes_model.json").exists() {

 // proceed with deserialization

} else {

 panic!("File not found");

}
```

#3 Memory Overflow

When training, especially k-NN, you might run into memory errors since the algorithm stores all the training data.

Solution

If you encounter a memory error, consider using dimensionality reduction techniques like PCA to reduce the memory footprint of your data. Alternatively, use a batch training method if your library supports it.

```
// Using PCA for dimensionality reduction

let reduced_data = pca.transform(data);

let knn_model = KNN::new(3);

knn_model.fit(&reduced_data, &labels);
```

#4 Poor Generalization

The model performs exceptionally well on the training data but poorly on unseen data.

Solution

This is a classic sign of overfitting. For k-NN, reducing the value of 'k' can sometimes improve generalization. For Naive Bayes, ensure that you have enough data and the features are not highly correlated.

```
// Reducing 'k' to combat overfitting in k-NN

let knn_model = KNN::new(1); // instead of KNN::new(5)
```

#5 Inconsistent Data Types

You might encounter errors related to inconsistent data types, especially when working with libraries that are strict about data types.

Solution

Do not forget to check the data types of all variables and convert them to the required format. Rust's type system is strict, so explicit type conversion might be necessary.

```
// Explicitly casting types if needed

let my_var: f64 = some_func() as f64;
```

#6 Data Imbalance for Classification

In both Naive Bayes and k-NN, if one class dominates the others in your dataset, the model will be biased.

Solution

You can either undersample the majority class, oversample the minority class, or use techniques like SMOTE for balancing the classes. Imbalanced classes can lead to misleadingly high accuracy.

```
// Using Rust libraries to balance data

let balanced_data = some_balance_func(data, labels);
```

#7 Feature Scaling

k-NN is highly sensitive to feature scaling, and having features on different scales can lead to poor performance.

Solution

Always scale your features before training a k-NN model. Naive Bayes is generally not affected by this, but it is a good practice.

```
// Scaling features for k-NN

let scaled_data = some_scaling_func(data);
```

#8 Concurrency Issues

When we are deploying your model in a multi-threaded application, you might run into concurrency issues.

Solution

Do not forget your model and the libraries we are using are thread-safe. If not, you can manage access to your model using locks or other synchronization primitives.

```
// Using Mutex for thread-safe model access

use std::sync::Mutex;

let model = Mutex::new(my_trained_model);
```

#9 Incorrect Label Encoding

Both Naive Bayes and k-NN require the labels to be encoded properly. Improper encoding might lead to unexpected behavior.

Solution

Always check the label encoding and, if required, use label encoding utilities to ensure that your labels are in the correct format.

```
// Properly encoding labels

let encoded_labels = label_encoder.transform(labels);
```

The key to successful machine learning projects in Rust, or any language, is understanding not only how to develop models, but also how to troubleshoot and refine them. This section on troubleshooting provides you with the solutions you need to create, analyze, and deploy reliable Naive Bayes and k-NN models in real-world applications.

Summary

In this chapter, we explored two fundamental but powerful machine learning algorithms: Naive Bayes and k-NN. We began by studying the design of Naive Bayes, which uses Bayes' theorem and a 'naive' assumption of feature independence to anticipate the target class. We also learned how k-NN works on the simple concept of feature similarity, making predictions based on the 'k' closest points in the feature space. Both methods have significant advantages and disadvantages, and the choice depends on the task at hand.

We next moved on to practical implementations, focusing on the heart prediction dataset. We used techniques like naive Bayes to build a classifier and adjust its parameters, such as the smoothing factor. For k-NN, we explored distance metrics and the significance of selecting the suitable 'k.' Both models were serialized and deserialized, illustrating the versatility and ease of model storage and retrieval. The adoption of libraries such as serde facilitated this process.

The chapter also addressed error identification and troubleshooting. From data imbalance to incorrect label encoding, we identified ten different types of defects that can occur while working with these models. We learned about Rust-specific obstacles, such as working with restricted data types and potential concurrency problems. Each issue was addressed in a practical manner, providing you with the tools required for effective debugging and model creation.

Finally, we compared Naive Bayes and k-NN on the same dataset to better understand the differences. This comparative analysis aimed to provide a better understanding of when to use which algorithm. We also briefly talked about hyperparameter tweaking and its function in improving model performance. This comprehensive method aimed to provide a broad understanding of these algorithms, from theory to practical application and debugging.

Chapter 9: Crafting Neural Networks with Rust

Introduction to Neural Networks

The journey through machine learning and its algorithms, culminating in the exploration of neural networks, represents a significant evolution in our quest to replicate and understand human intelligence. This progression from simple linear models to complex neural architectures reflects our growing computational capabilities and deeper theoretical insights. Neural networks, a cornerstone of modern artificial intelligence (AI), have transformed the landscape of machine learning, pushing the boundaries of what machines can learn and achieve.

Genesis of Neural Networks

The concept of neural networks isn't new; it traces back to the 1940s and 1950s with the pioneering work of Warren McCulloch and Walter Pitts. They introduced a simplified model of the human neuron, proposing that networks of such artificial neurons could potentially learn and perform complex tasks. This idea was revolutionary, laying the foundational stone for neural network research. However, the computational resources and theoretical understanding at the time were insufficient to realize their full potential.

Neural networks experienced periods of both fervent interest and relative obscurity, often referred to as the "AI winters," when skepticism and funding shortages hampered research. Despite these challenges, key developments kept the field advancing. The backpropagation algorithm, introduced in the 1980s, for instance, enabled more effective training of multi-layer networks by efficiently computing gradients. Yet, it wasn't until the advent of big data and substantial improvements in computational power, particularly through GPUs, that neural networks began to show their true capabilities.

Breakthroughs and Modern Applications

The discovery of neural networks as a real technology was solidified by breakthroughs in deep learning in the early 2010s. Researchers demonstrated that deep neural networks, containing many layers of neurons, could achieve unprecedented performance on tasks like image recognition, speech recognition, and natural language processing. The success of AlexNet in the 2012 ImageNet competition was a watershed moment, showcasing the superiority of deep neural networks in image classification tasks and reinvigorating the field of AI.

These advancements were made possible by a confluence of factors. Firstly, the availability of large datasets allowed neural networks to learn from a vast array of examples, essential for their ability to generalize well to new, unseen data. Secondly, GPUs provided the necessary computational power to train deep networks, which require significant computational resources due to their complexity and the large number of parameters. Finally, innovations in neural network architecture, training algorithms, and regularization techniques have continually improved their performance and capabilities.

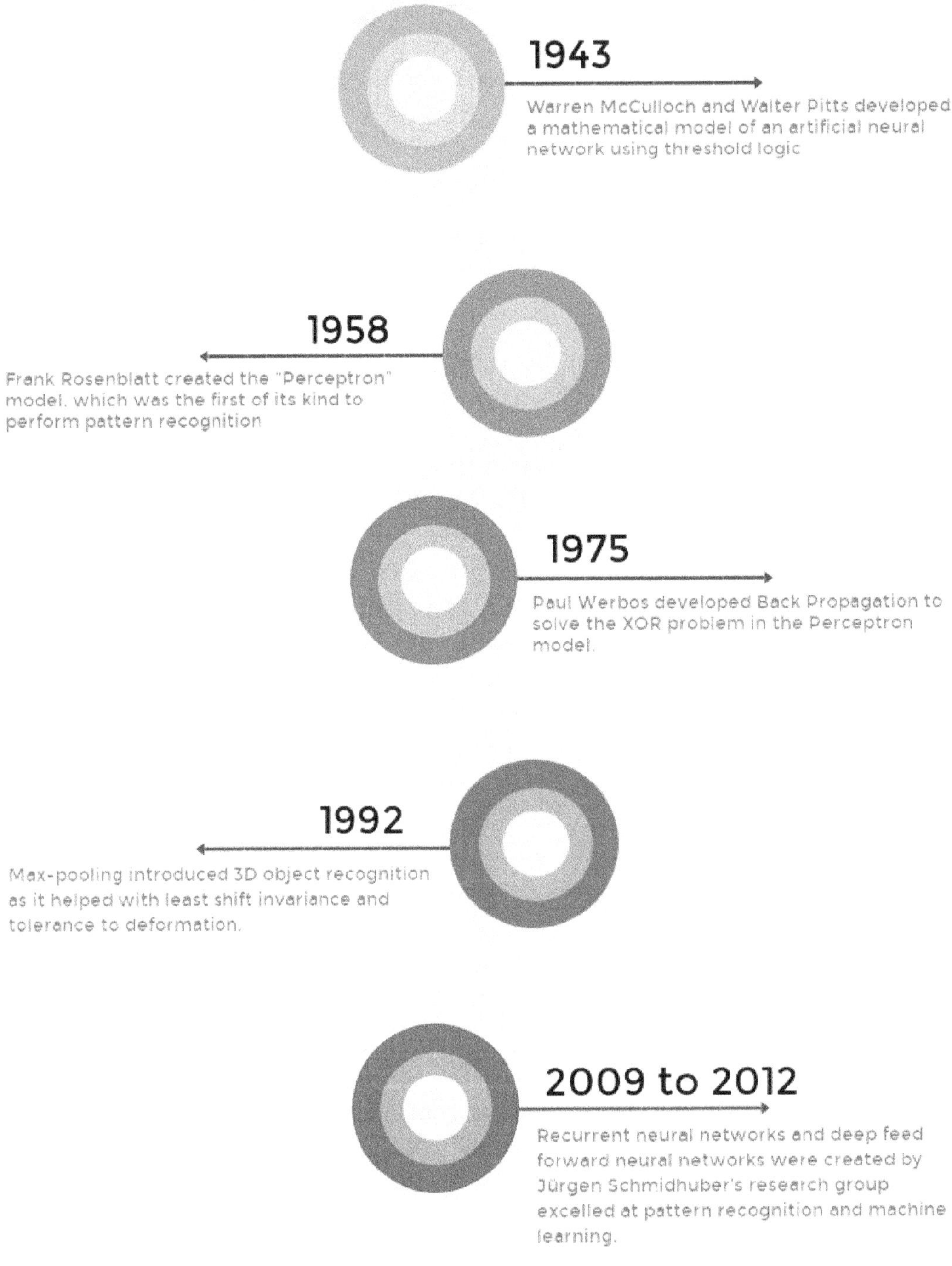

Fig 9.1 History of Neural Networks

Neural Networks in Today's World

Today, neural networks are at the heart of numerous applications that were once thought to be the exclusive domain of human intelligence. From autonomous vehicles and advanced medical diagnoses to sophisticated language translation services and content recommendation systems, neural networks have become ubiquitous in technology that impacts daily life. Their ability to learn hierarchical representations of data, capturing both low-level features and high-level abstractions, makes them exceptionally versatile and powerful.

The evolution into the new world of neural networks represents a significant milestone in machine learning and AI. It embodies the culmination of decades of research, technological advancements, and a deeper understanding of both artificial and natural intelligence. Neural networks have not only expanded the horizons of what's possible with machine learning but have also provided a computational model that mirrors some aspects of human cognitive processes.

Components of Neural Networks

Neural networks are composed of several key ingredients that work in concert to enable them to learn from data and make predictions or decisions. Understanding the below components is crucial to dive into neural networks, whether in Rust or Python or any other programming language.

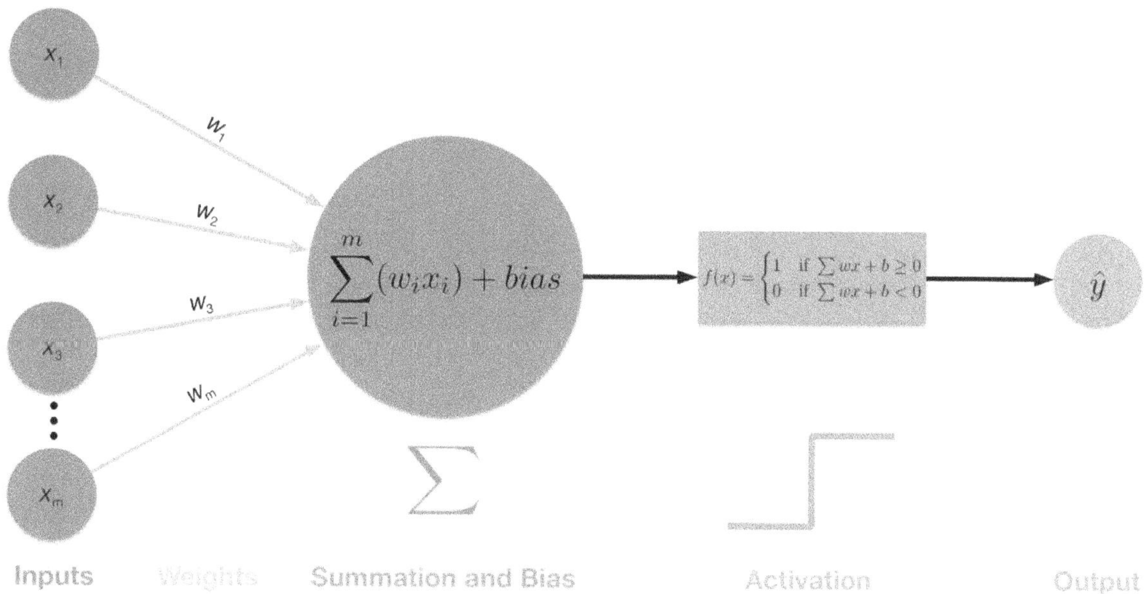

Fig 9.2 Neural Network Components

Neurons

Neurons, also known as nodes, are the fundamental building blocks of neural networks. These nodes are modeled after the real neurons that are found in the human brain. Every neuron takes in information, processes it, and then transmits the results of its processing to the subsequent layer of neurons. In most cases, the processing phase begins with the application of an activation function, which is then followed by a weighted sum of the inputs.

Layers

The input layer, one or more hidden layers, and the output layer are the layers that are used to organize neurons (neuron organization). A number of computations are carried out by the hidden layers, the input layer is responsible for receiving the initial data, and the output layer is responsible for producing the final prediction or classification.

Weight and Biases

An associated weight is assigned to every connection that exists between neurons, and every neuron possesses a bias. In the course of its training, the neural network acquires knowledge of these parameters, which include weights and biases. Adjustments are made to them in order to reduce the amount of variance that exists between the predictions made by the network and the actual target values.

Activation Functions

Activation functions present the network with non-linearity, which enables the network to acquire the ability to learn intricate patterns. For the output layer of classification tasks, some of the activation functions that are commonly used include the sigmoid, tanh, ReLU (Rectified Linear Unit), and softmax.

Loss Function

The difference between the output that was projected for the network and the output that actually occurred is what the loss function, also known as the cost function, quantifies. The objective of the training is to reduce this loss as much as possible. As an illustration, the mean squared error is utilized for regression activities, and cross-entropy loss is utilized for classification jobs.

Optimizer

In order to reduce the amount of loss, the optimizer is the algorithm that is used to alter the weights and biases in the appropriate direction. In practice, versions of gradient descent like as SGD (Stochastic Gradient Descent), Adam, and RMSprop are frequently utilized. Gradient descent is a foundational approach to optimization.

Backpropagation

In this manner, the neural network acquires knowledge and develops its capabilities. Through the use of the chain rule, backpropagation is able to compute the gradient of the loss function with respect to each weight and bias. This provides the optimizer with the ability to update the parameters in an appropriate manner.

NeuroFlow for Neural Networks

NeuroFlow is a Rust library designed for building and training neural networks. It leverages Rust's performance and safety features to provide an efficient and user-friendly interface for machine learning applications. With NeuroFlow, users can construct neural networks with various architectures, including feedforward and convolutional networks, customize layers, activation functions, and optimizers, and train their models with a straightforward API.

To start using NeuroFlow in your Rust project, you would typically add it to your Cargo.toml file as a dependency. Then, you can begin defining your neural network model, layer by layer, specifying the desired activation functions and other hyperparameters. NeuroFlow abstracts away much of the complexity involved in manually implementing forward and backward passes, gradient computations, and parameter updates, making it accessible for Rust developers to experiment with neural networks.

In the subsequent sections, we will dive deeper into how to use NeuroFlow to create a neural network, focusing on constructing the network architecture, preparing the data, training the model, and evaluating its performance, all within the Rust programming environment. This approach will not only highlight the practical aspects of working with neural networks but also demonstrate the power and flexibility of NeuroFlow for machine learning tasks.

Install NeuroFlow

The below step-by-step directions will give you a better solution on which to install and configure NeuroFlow for your deep learning projects.

Adding NeuroFlow to Rust Project

First, you need to include NeuroFlow in your Rust project's Cargo.toml file. Assuming NeuroFlow is available as a crate, you would add it under [dependencies] like so:

```
[dependencies]

neuroflow = "x.y.z"
```

Replace "x.y.z" with the latest version of NeuroFlow. After saving the Cargo.toml file, run cargo build in your terminal to download and compile the NeuroFlow crate along with its dependencies.

Creating Single-Layer Neural Network

Creating a neural network involves defining the network structure and specifying parameters like the number of input features, the number of neurons in the layer(s), the activation function, and the learning rate. A single-layer neural network, also known as a perceptron, can serve as a linear classifier.

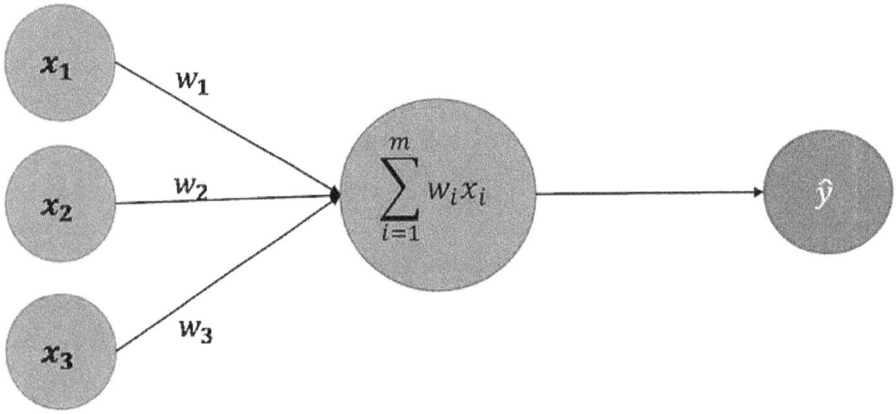

Fig 9.3 Single Layer Neural Network

First, you need to import the necessary components from NeuroFlow. Then, you can define the network:

```
extern crate neuroflow;

use neuroflow::FeedForward;

use neuroflow::activators::Sigmoid;

use neuroflow::data::DataSet;

fn main() {

 // Define the network architecture

 let mut net = FeedForward::new(&[2, 1]); // 2 inputs, 1 output neuron

 net.activator(Sigmoid); // Using Sigmoid activation function for output neuron

  // Create a dataset

 // Assuming we have a binary classification task with inputs as [f32; 2] and outputs as
[f32; 1]
```

```
let data = DataSet::new(
vec![vec![0.0, 0.0], vec![1.0, 1.0], vec![1.0, 0.0], vec![0.0, 1.0]], // Inputs
vec![vec![0.0], vec![0.0], vec![1.0], vec![1.0]] // Corresponding outputs
);
 // Train the network
// Assuming a learning rate of 0.1 and 10000 epochs
net.train(&data, 0.1, 10000).expect("Failed to train the network");
 // Test the network
let test_input = vec![1.0, 0.0];
let prediction = net.run(&test_input).expect("Failed to run the network");
println!("Prediction: {:?}", prediction);
}
```

In the above code snippet,

- The array [2, 1] passed to FeedForward::new specifies that the network should have two input neurons and one output neuron.
- The Sigmoid function is chosen because it outputs values between 0 and 1, making it suitable for binary classification tasks.
- The train function takes the dataset, a learning rate, and the number of epochs as arguments. The learning rate controls how much we adjust the weights with respect to the loss gradient, and the number of epochs specifies how many times the entire dataset will be passed through the network.
- The run function is used to feed new data through the trained network and obtain predictions.

From the above code, a very basic single-layer neural network is created with two input features and one output neuron using the Sigmoid activation function. This setup could be used for a simple binary classification task. The DataSet::new function is used to create training data, where each input vector corresponds to an output vector. The `train` method is then used to train the network with the specified learning rate and number of epochs. Finally, the `run` method is used to make a prediction for a test input.

There may be some subtle differences in the syntax and functions available in NeuroFlow, but the core ideas behind designing the network, choosing an activation function, and training the network are uniform.

PyTorch for Neural Networks

PyTorch has emerged as one of the top deep learning libraries, providing both flexibility and capability when creating and training neural networks. Its appeal among researchers and developers originates from its straightforward design, ease of use, and dynamic computational graph, which provides greater flexibility when developing complex models. PyTorch also has a robust ecosystem of tools for deep learning research, including model construction, training, and deployment.

Core Features of PyTorch

Dynamic computational graph

PyTorch uses dynamic computational graphs, as opposed to static graphs used by certain other tools. This allows for dynamic updates and makes the graph more intuitive by building it on the fly as operations are executed. This is very useful for debugging and models that use conditional operations and loops.

Simplicity and Flexibility

PyTorch's API is designed to be as near to the Python programming language as possible, making it easy to learn but still powerful enough for research. It enables easy model definition, maintenance, and extension.

Strong GPU Acceleration

PyTorch supports CUDA seamlessly, enabling for efficient calculation on GPUs. This greatly accelerates the training and inference procedures, allowing for the use of big datasets and complicated models.

Extensive Libraries

A wide variety of libraries and tools are available to support PyTorch. Some of them are torchvision, which processes images, torchaudio, which processes audio, and torchtext, which processes natural language. These libraries offer pre-built datasets, model structures, and common procedures, making it easier to construct complex models.

TorchScript for Easy Deployment

PyTorch provides TorchScript, a tool for converting PyTorch models into a format that runs independently of Python. This is very handy when delivering models in production contexts where Python might not be available.

Creating a Neural Network in PyTorch

Creating a neural network in PyTorch involves defining a model class by extending the torch.nn.Module class, specifying the layers in the __init__ method, and defining the forward pass in the forward method. Given below is a simple example:

```
import torch

import torch.nn as nn

import torch.nn.functional as F

class SimpleNN(nn.Module):

def __init__(self):

super(SimpleNN, self).__init__()

self.fc1 = nn.Linear(784, 128) # First layer: 784 inputs, 128 outputs

self.fc2 = nn.Linear(128, 10) # Second layer: 128 inputs, 10 outputs (for 10 classes)

def forward(self, x):

x = F.relu(self.fc1(x)) # Activation function for first layer

x = self.fc2(x) # Output layer

return F.log softmax(x, dim=1) # Log Softmax activation for output
```

The above sample program defines a simple feedforward neural network for classification with one hidden layer. The model uses the ReLU activation function for the hidden layer and a log softmax function for the output layer, suitable for a multi-class classification problem.

Training a Model in PyTorch

Training a model involves defining a loss function, an optimizer, and writing a training loop. The loss function (torch.nn.CrossEntropyLoss for classification tasks) measures how well the model's predictions match the target labels. The optimizer (e.g., torch.optim.Adam) adjusts the model's weights based on the gradients to minimize the loss.

```
loss_function = nn.CrossEntropyLoss()

optimizer = torch.optim.Adam(model.parameters(), lr=0.001)

for epoch in range(num_epochs):

 for inputs, labels in train_loader: # Assuming you have a DataLoader

 optimizer.zero_grad() # Clear existing gradients

 outputs = model(inputs) # Forward pass

 loss = loss_function(outputs, labels) # Compute loss

 loss.backward() # Backward pass

 optimizer.step() # Update model parameters
```

Using PyTorch in Rust

Integrating PyTorch models in Rust applications typically involves exporting the trained model from PyTorch using TorchScript and then loading the model . This process requires a Rust library that can interface with TorchScript, such as tch-rs, which provides Rust bindings for PyTorch.

Exporting PyTorch Model with TorchScript

```
# Assuming model is your trained PyTorch model

scripted_model = torch.jit.script(model)

scripted_model.save("model.pt")
```

Using Model with tch-rs

First, add tch-rs to your Cargo.toml:

```
[dependencies]

tch = "0.4.1"
```

Then, you can load and use the model:

```
extern crate tch;

use tch::{CModule, Tensor};


fn main() {

 let model = CModule::load("model.pt").unwrap();

 let tensor = Tensor::randn(&[1, 784], tch::Kind::Float, tch::Device::Cpu); // Example input tensor

 let output = model.forward_ts(&[tensor]).unwrap();

 println!("{:?}", output);

}
```

The above sample program demonstrates loading a TorchScript model and performing a forward pass with a random input tensor. Ensure that **tch-rs** requires LibTorch, the PyTorch C++ library, to be installed in your environment.

Through this approach, you can leverage PyTorch's powerful deep learning capabilities within Rust applications, combining PyTorch's ease of model development and training with Rust's performance and safety features. This synergy allows for the efficient deployment of machine learning models in production environments where Rust's system-level control is beneficial.

Setup LibTorch

A number of steps are involved in installing LibTorch on a Linux environment and making sure it can be accessed for running Rust programs. In general, you will follow these steps, however they may differ slightly based on your particular Linux distribution and implementation:

Download LibTorch

First, go to the PyTorch official website or the specific URL where the LibTorch binaries are provided. Select the version of LibTorch that matches your requirements (CPU or GPU version) and download the zip file. For example:

wget https://download.pytorch.org/libtorch/cpu/libtorch-shared-with-deps-latest.zip

Extract LibTorch Archive

Once the download is complete, extract the zip file to a directory of your choice. A common practice is to place it in /usr/local/lib or a directory within your home folder, depending on whether you want to make LibTorch available system-wide or just for your user. For system-wide installation, you might need sudo permissions.

unzip libtorch-shared-with-deps-latest.zip -d /usr/local/lib/

Set Environment Variables

To ensure that the Rust compiler and linker can find LibTorch, you need to set the LIBTORCH and LD_LIBRARY_PATH environment variables. You can set these variables in your .bashrc, .zshrc, or another shell configuration file, depending on which shell you use.

echo 'export LIBTORCH=/usr/local/lib/libtorch' >> ~/.bashrc

echo 'export
LD_LIBRARY_PATH=/usr/local/lib/libtorch/lib:$LD_LIBRARY_PATH' >>
~/.bashrc

source ~/.bashrc

This sets LIBTORCH to the directory where you extracted LibTorch and adds LibTorch's lib directory to your LD_LIBRARY_PATH, which helps the dynamic linker find the LibTorch libraries.

Install tch-rs Crate

With LibTorch installed and the environment variables set, you can proceed to add tch-rs to your Rust project by including it in your Cargo.toml file:

```
[dependencies]

tch = "0.4.1"
```

Then, run `cargo build` in your project directory. Cargo will download and compile the `tch-rs` crate along with its dependencies. The `tch-rs` crate will automatically find the LibTorch installation using the environment variables you set.

Verify Installation

To verify that everything is set up correctly, you can write a simple Rust program that loads a TorchScript model or performs a tensor operation using `tch-rs`, as demonstrated previously.

```
extern crate tch;

use tch::Tensor;

fn main() {

 let tensor = Tensor::randn(&[2, 3], tch::Kind::Float, tch::Device::Cpu);

 println!("{:?}", tensor);

}
```

Running this program with `cargo run` should execute without errors, indicating that `tch-rs` can successfully use the LibTorch libraries.

Building Multi-Layer Neural Networks or MLPs

Diving deeper into the realm of neural networks, we transition from the simplicity of single-layer architectures to the more complex and powerful multi-layer neural networks, often referred to as Multi-Layer Perceptrons (MLPs). These networks consist of one input layer, multiple hidden layers, and one output layer, with each layer containing a set of neurons or nodes. The addition of hidden layers enables the network to learn higher-level features in data, capturing complex patterns that are not possible with single-layer networks. This capability makes MLPs suitable for a wide range of tasks including image recognition, speech processing, and natural language understanding.

Understanding Multi-Layer Neural Networks

The key to MLPs' effectiveness lies in their architecture. Each neuron in a layer connects to every neuron in the subsequent layer, forming a dense network of connections. Information flows from the input layer through the hidden layers to the output layer. The hidden layers allow MLPs to construct hierarchical representations of the input data. The first hidden layer might learn simple features, such as edges in an image, while deeper layers combine these features to detect more complex patterns, such as shapes or objects.

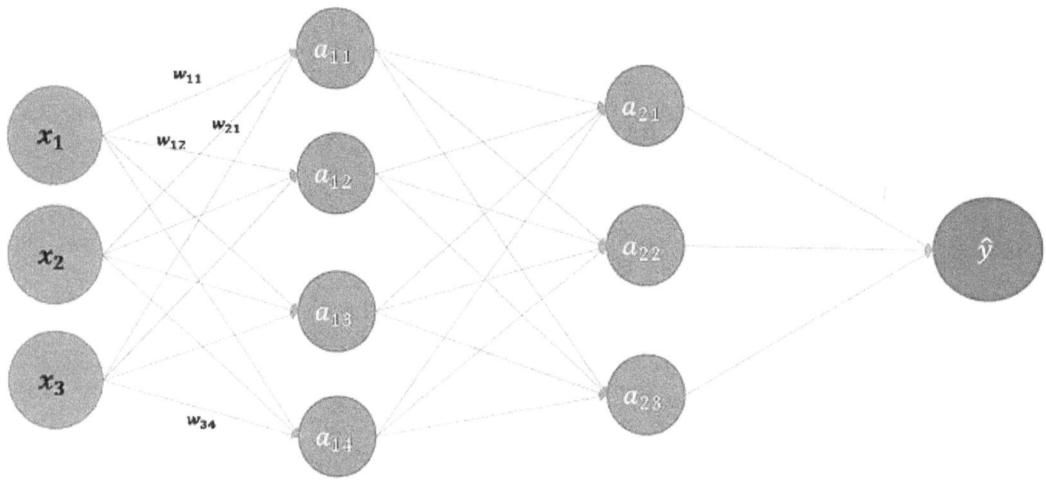

Fig 9.4 Multi-Layer Perceptron

Activation functions play a crucial role in MLPs by introducing non-linearity into the network. Without non-linear activation functions like ReLU (Rectified Linear Unit) or Sigmoid, stacking multiple layers wouldn't increase the network's ability to model complex relationships, as the composition of linear functions is itself a linear function.

Using PyTorch to build Multi-Layer Neural Network

PyTorch's modular design simplifies the process of building and training MLPs, allowing you to specify custom neural network topologies using the torch.nn. Module class. Below is how to use a basic MLP to a classification task:

```
import torch

import torch.nn as nn

import torch.nn.functional as F

class MultiLayerPerceptron(nn.Module):
```

```
def __init__(self):
super(MultiLayerPerceptron, self).__init__()
# Define the first hidden layer
self.hidden1 = nn.Linear(in_features=784, out_features=128)
# Define the second hidden layer
self.hidden2 = nn.Linear(128, 64)
# Define the output layer
self.output = nn.Linear(64, 10)
# Define an activation function
self.relu = nn.ReLU()
def forward(self, x):
# Pass data through the first hidden layer and apply activation
x = self.relu(self.hidden1(x))
# Pass data through the second hidden layer and apply activation
x = self.relu(self.hidden2(x))
# Pass data through the output layer
x = self.output(x)
return x
```

In the above code snippet, the MultiLayerPerceptron class defines a neural network with two hidden layers and one output layer. The input to the network is expected to be a flattened image of size 784 (28x28 pixels), making this network suitable for tasks like digit classification from the MNIST dataset. The network outputs 10 values corresponding to the scores for each class.

Training a Multi-Layer Neural Network

Training an MLP involves defining a loss function and an optimizer, then iterating over the dataset in batches, performing forward and backward passes, and updating the model's weights. Given below is a simplified training loop:

```
# Assume train_loader is a DataLoader object for your training data

# Define a loss function

criterion = nn.CrossEntropyLoss()

# Define an optimizer

optimizer = torch.optim.Adam(model.parameters(), lr=0.001)

# Iterate over epochs

for epoch in range(epochs):

 for inputs, labels in train_loader:

 # Zero the parameter gradients

 optimizer.zero_grad()

 # Forward pass

 outputs = model(inputs)

 loss = criterion(outputs, labels)

 # Backward pass and optimize

 loss.backward()

 optimizer.step()
```

This training procedure enables the MLP to iteratively alter its parameters (weights and biases) in order to reduce the difference between its predictions and the actual labels, resulting in effective learning to categorize input data. MLPs can learn deep representations of input data by stacking layers and utilizing non-linear activation functions, making them extremely useful for a variety of machine learning tasks.

Using ndarray for MLP

If you're not interested in using the previously learnt machine learning frameworks, NeuroFlow or PyTorch, you can still build a neural network or an MLP using Rust's ndarray library. ndarray provides powerful, multidimensional arrays that facilitate numerical computations and operations crucial for building neural networks from scratch. This approach demands a deeper understanding of the neural network's mechanics, including manual implementation of forward propagation, backpropagation, and weight updates. We approach this process with an emphasis on precision and thoroughness as below:

Up and Running with ndarray

First, ensure ndarray is included in your project's Cargo.toml:

```
[dependencies]

ndarray = "0.15.3"
```

The version may vary; always seek the latest version compatible with your project. ndarray will serve as the backbone for our data structures, enabling efficient matrix operations that are essential for neural network computations.

Defining MLP Structure

Constructing an MLP involves initializing the weights and biases for each layer, defining the activation function, and preparing for forward and backward propagation. Given below is a simplified structure, assuming a two-hidden-layer MLP for our learning purpose:

```
extern crate ndarray;

use ndarray::Array2; // Import Array2 for 2D arrays

struct MultiLayerPerceptron {

 // Layer weights

 weights1: Array2<f32>,

 weights2: Array2<f32>,
```

```
weights3: Array2<f32>,

// Layer biases

bias1: Array2<f32>,

bias2: Array2<f32>,

bias3: Array2<f32>,

}

impl MultiLayerPerceptron {

fn new(input_size: usize, hidden1_size: usize, hidden2_size: usize, output_size: usize) ->
MultiLayerPerceptron {

let mut rng = rand::thread_rng();

// Initialize weights and biases with random values

// For simplicity, random values are in the range [-0.5, 0.5], adjust as needed

MultiLayerPerceptron {

weights1: Array2::random((input_size, hidden1_size), -0.5..0.5),

weights2: Array2::random((hidden1_size, hidden2_size), -0.5..0.5),

weights3: Array2::random((hidden2_size, output_size), -0.5..0.5),

bias1: Array2::zeros((1, hidden1_size)),

bias2: Array2::zeros((1, hidden2_size)),

bias3: Array2::zeros((1, output_size)),

}

}
```

```
// Define forward propagation, activation functions, backpropagation, and training methods here

}
```

Forward Propagation

The forward propagation method calculates the output for a given input by sequentially passing data through the network's layers. Each layer's output becomes the next layer's input, with an activation function applied at each step.

```
use ndarray::Array;

use ndarray_rand::RandomExt;

use ndarray_rand::rand_distr::Uniform;

fn relu(x: &Array2<f32>) -> Array2<f32> {

 x.mapv(|a| a.max(0.0))

}

fn softmax(x: &Array2<f32>) -> Array2<f32> {

 let exp_x = x.mapv(|a| a.exp());

 &exp_x / exp_x.sum_axis(ndarray::Axis(1)).insert_axis(ndarray::Axis(1))

}

impl MultiLayerPerceptron {

 fn forward(&self, inputs: &Array2<f32>) -> Array2<f32> {

 let z1 = inputs.dot(&self.weights1) + &self.bias1;

 let a1 = relu(&z1);

 let z2 = a1.dot(&self.weights2) + &self.bias2;
```

```
let a2 = relu(&z2);

let z3 = a2.dot(&self.weights3) + &self.bias3;

softmax(&z3) // Assuming a classification problem

}

}
```

The next stage is obvious: training. This training approach relies on backpropagation and gradient descent, which require calculating the gradient of the loss function with respect to each parameter. It involves modifying the weights and biases based on the error between the expected and actual outputs. This is beyond the scope of this book since it is quite complex and calls for a higher level of statistical and mathematical understanding.

Building a neural network with Rust using ndarray for computations exemplifies the blend of Rust's performance capabilities with the foundational principles of machine learning. Libraries such as ndarray may not come with built-in support for neural networks, but they let programmers build efficient machine learning models that are perfect for their projects, which opens up a world of possibilities for advancements in Rust-based ML.

Convolutional Neural Networks (CNNs)

CNNs are a major step forward in the field of deep learning, particularly for image processing applications like image recognition, classification, and object detection. Unlike the completely connected layers of a standard neural network or MLP, which we have learnt so far, CNNs introduce the concepts of convolutions, pooling, and spatial hierarchy, all of which are critical in dealing with high-dimensional input like images.

Understanding Convolutions

The basic principle behind convolutions in the context of CNNs is to apply a filter or kernel to the input data in order to extract meaningful features. As part of a convolution process, the filter is moved across the input picture and the dot product of the input pixels in the receptive field and the filter weights is computed. This procedure creates a feature map that highlights elements recognized by the filter, such as edges, textures, or specific forms. Convolutional layers enable CNNs to learn increasingly complicated patterns in data as the depth grows.

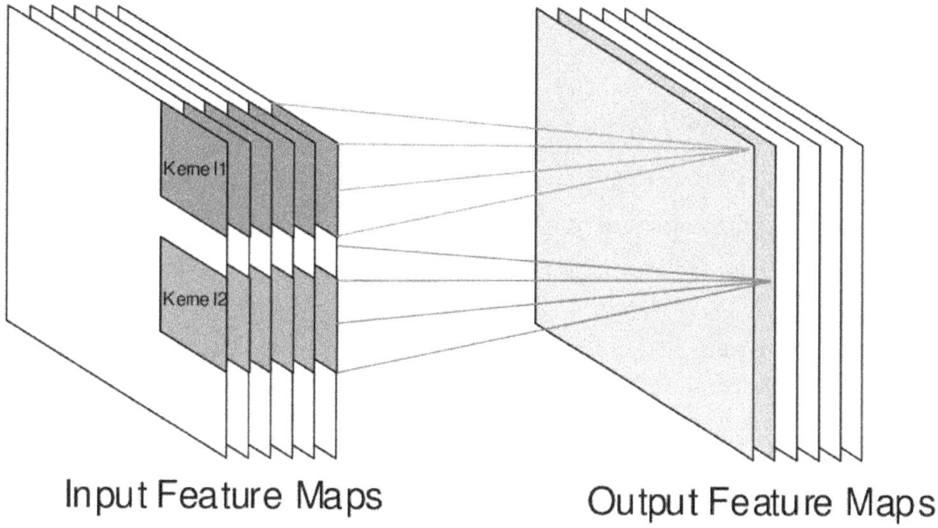

Fig 9.5 Convolutional Neural Network

Differentiation from Traditional Neural Networks

The primary difference between CNNs and previously learnt NNs is how they process data. Traditional NNs handle input data as flat, one-dimensional arrays, resulting in a loss of spatial and structural links found in images. CNNs use convolutions to preserve the spatial hierarchy and relationships within the data, allowing them to efficiently process and learn from visual data. Furthermore, CNNs greatly minimize the number of parameters necessary due to weight sharing and sparse connectivity, lowering the danger of overfitting and computational load.

Convolutional Neural Network Architecture

A CNN's architecture is made up of various layers, each of which serves a distinct function in the feature extraction and learning process:

Convolutional Layers

These layers serve as the backbone of CNNs, applying a set of learnable filters to the input. Each filter is tiny in size (width and height), yet it stretches throughout the entire depth of the input volume. In the early layers, the convolutional process catches patterns like as edges, while deeper layers' record more complicated information (such as object components).

Activation Layers

After each convolutional process, an activation function, such as the Rectified Linear Unit (ReLU), is applied. The goal of ReLU is to add nonlinearity to the model, allowing it to learn complex patterns.

Pooling Layers

Pooling (typically max pooling) layers are placed between subsequent convolutional layers to gradually lower the spatial size of the representation, reduce the number of parameters and computations in the network, and hence control overfitting. Max pooling selects the maximum element from the region of the feature map that the filter covers.

Fully Connected Layers

Following multiple convolutional and max-pooling layers, the neural network's high-level reasoning is carried out using fully connected layers. A CNN terminates with one or more completely connected layers, with the final fully connected layer containing the output, such as class scores in classification tasks. The outputs of the convolutional/pooling layers are flattened into a vector and fed into fully connected layers.

Dropout Layers

To reduce the danger of overfitting, dropout layers can be introduced shortly before the fully linked layer. During training, dropout layers randomly disregard a subset of neurons, making the network less sensitive to the weights of individual neurons.

Normalization Layers

Batch Normalization layers are frequently used after convolutional or fully connected layers to stabilize and speed up deep network training. They operate by normalizing the inputs to a layer for each mini-batch, keeping the mean output near to zero and the output standard deviation close to one.

Application in Real World

In real-world applications, a convolutional neural network (CNN) may apply a series of convolutional and max pooling layers successively to an input image. This network component is in charge of feature extraction, which involves recognizing patterns in a picture that are relevant to the task at hand, such as image classification. The fully linked layers that follow serve as a classifier on top of the features.

CNNs have transformed the field of computer vision, performing admirably in tasks that were previously difficult for machines. Their ability to automatically and adaptively learn spatial hierarchies of information from images makes them ideal for image and video identification, image classification, medical image analysis, and even playing critical roles in self-driving systems.

The development of CNNs was a watershed moment in deep learning, delivering a tool capable of capturing detailed patterns in visual data and making sense of the complicated world around us in a manner that resembles the efficiency and precision of the human visual system. The transition from simple neural networks to CNNs exemplifies a larger trend in machine learning and AI: the shift toward models that not only handle raw data but also analyze it in fundamentally humanistic ways.

Building CNN using PyTorch

Now that we have a sufficient grasp of neural networks and what makes CNNs unique, we can use PyTorch to build one. In this section, we will lead you through an actual program that defines a CNN architecture appropriate for a simple image classification task, such as discriminating between different sorts of objects in the CIFAR-10 dataset, which has 60,000 32x32 color images divided into ten groups. You may download the dataset from:

https://www.cs.toronto.edu/~kriz/cifar-10-python.tar.gz

Define CNN Architecture

You first define your model by subclassing **nn.Module** and initializing the neural network layers in the constructor. You then specify how data will pass through the network in the **forward** method. We define a basic CNN:

```
import torch

import torch.nn as nn

import torch.nn.functional as F



class SimpleCNN(nn.Module):

 def __init__(self):

 super(SimpleCNN, self).__init__()

 # Convolutional layer (sees 32x32x3 image tensor)

 self.conv1 = nn.Conv2d(in_channels=3, out_channels=16, kernel_size=3, stride=1,
padding=1)

 # Convolutional layer (sees 16x16x16 tensor)

 self.conv2 = nn.Conv2d(16, 32, 3, 1, 1)
```

```
# Convolutional layer (sees 8x8x32 tensor)
self.conv3 = nn.Conv2d(32, 64, 3, 1, 1)
# Max pooling
self.pool = nn.MaxPool2d(2, 2)
# Linear layer (64 * 4 * 4 = 1024)
self.fc1 = nn.Linear(64 * 4 * 4, 512)
# Linear layer (512 -> 10)
self.fc2 = nn.Linear(512, 10)
# Dropout layer (p=0.2)
self.dropout = nn.Dropout(0.2)
def forward(self, x):
# Add sequence of convolutional and max pooling layers
x = self.pool(F.relu(self.conv1(x)))
x = self.pool(F.relu(self.conv2(x)))
x = self.pool(F.relu(self.conv3(x)))
# Flatten image input
x = x.view(-1, 64 * 4 * 4)
# Add dropout layer
x = self.dropout(x)
# Add 1st hidden layer, with relu activation function
x = F.relu(self.fc1(x))
```

```
# Add dropout layer

x = self.dropout(x)

# Add 2nd hidden layer, with relu activation function

x = self.fc2(x)

return x
```

This CNN architecture begins with three convolutional layers, each followed by a ReLU activation function and a max pooling layer to reduce the spatial dimensions of the output tensor. After the convolutional layers, the tensor is flattened, and then it is passed through two linear (fully connected) layers to classify the images into 10 categories. Dropout layers are added to prevent overfitting.

Initialize Model and Specify Loss Function/Optimizer

Once your CNN architecture is defined, you need to create an instance of your model, specify a loss function, and select an optimizer for training.

```
model = SimpleCNN()

criterion = nn.CrossEntropyLoss()

optimizer = torch.optim.Adam(model.parameters(), lr=0.001)
```

Train the Model

Training involves iterating over the dataset, making predictions with your model, and updating the model's weights based on the loss calculated from the true labels and the predictions.

```
# Assume you have a DataLoader for your training data: train_loader



epochs = 10 # Define the number of epochs



for epoch in range(epochs):
```

```
running_loss = 0.0
for images, labels in train_loader:
# Zero the parameter gradients
optimizer.zero_grad()
# Forward pass
outputs = model(images)
loss = criterion(outputs, labels)
 # Backward pass and optimize
loss.backward()
optimizer.step()
 running_loss += loss.item()
 print(f"Epoch {epoch+1}, Loss: {running_loss/len(train_loader)}")
```

This simple training loop demonstrates the essential process: for each epoch, you loop through the dataset, compute the loss for each batch, and update the model parameters (**weights** and **biases**). Ensure that you will manage the data's shape and type to match your model's input requirements, typically requiring normalization and possibly reshaping of the input data.

The preceding example is simply a starting point for exploring more complex models, deeper architectures, and advanced approaches such as regularization, batch normalization, and more powerful optimizers to address picture recognition difficulties.

Summary

Deep learning, a subset of machine learning, is a huge discipline with many more topics and specialties than we've covered in this book. As we conclude our journey, it is crucial to note the wide range of topics within deep learning that await your curiosity and passion. Subjects like Generative Adversarial Networks (GANs) provide unique insights into generating new data instances that mimic your training data, which can be used in picture production, video synthesis, and other applications. Reinforcement Learning (RL) is an environment-agent interaction model in which algorithms learn to make decisions by performing actions in an environment to achieve certain goals. It is important in game theory, robotics, and navigation systems.

Attention mechanisms and transformers have transformed natural language processing (NLP), allowing for breakthroughs in machine translation, text summarization, and question-answering systems. These models, which focus on the relevance of input portions to a job, have resulted in the development of models such as BERT and GPT, which are pushing the boundaries of AI's ability to interpret and generate human-like language. Furthermore, self-supervised learning, a paradigm in which models learn from data that is not explicitly labeled, is gaining popularity due to its efficiency and capacity to harness massive amounts of unannotated information.

In this chapter, we explored CNN architecture and how it differs from simpler neural network models. By building a CNN with PyTorch and applying it to an image classification task, we've created the groundwork for understanding how deep learning may be used to analyze and handle visual data. The process of creating neural networks underlined the versatility and durability of deep learning, demonstrating how these concepts can be applied across many programming environments. This exploration is only the beginning; the area of deep learning is constantly changing, with new models, techniques, and applications emerging at an unparalleled speed. As you go, use your curiosity to navigate you through the enormous canvas of deep learning, discovering ideas that ignite your interest and drive innovation.

Epilogue

Thinking back on our time together as we close the book on our exploration of the Rust and machine learning worlds, I feel a sense of accomplishment. This book was written to be a guide for people who are interested in how the strength of Rust and the flexibility of machine learning can work together. Right from the start, our goal was clear and bold: to find new areas where precise code meets strong prediction. Now that I'm the author, I'm not at the end, but at a high point, giving both a review of our trip and some thoughts on the road ahead.

In these pages, we've gone over the basic ideas behind Rust and looked into how machine learning methods work, from simple models to the complex architecture of neural networks. Each part wasn't written to be an all-inclusive guide, but as a collection of learning opportunities meant to spark interest and lead to more research. We've seen how the speed and safety features of Rust can be used to solve problems in machine learning. These real-world examples can be used as both instructions and ideas.

But it's important to be careful and aware as you walk this road. As was already said, this book is not the only way to learn machine learning with Rust. Instead, it is meant to be a guide for your research. Getting better at something is a long and difficult process. Rust and machine learning are both areas that change quickly. What seems like a new idea today might be surpassed tomorrow. It's important to go into this journey with the mindset that you will always be learning and changing.

Also, even though we've talked about a lot of different techniques and uses, keep in mind that the best way to learn is to try things out and see what works. The cases and datasets given, like COVID, CIFAR-10, and others, are just places to start. I want you to try these ideas out on new problems, look into different sets of data, and go beyond what you think is possible.

Finally, I want you to think of this book not as the end of your learning journey but as a way to start exploring the vast, uncharted seas of Rust and machine learning. Take on the difficulties and unknowns with the attitude of a student, and let your curiosity guide you. Remember that the learning group is active and helpful if you run into problems or find things that need more explanation. Please don't be afraid to email support@gitforgits.com to share your thoughts and get help.

As we say goodbye in writing, keep in mind that the search for truth is never really over. The combination of Rust and machine learning has a huge amount of potential that is just ready to be discovered. Keep up the spirit of asking questions, coming up with new ideas, and working together. May your way be lit up with new insights, breakthroughs, and successes. Thanks for going with me on this trip. Let's keep learning, exploring, and coming up with new ideas, because the future is bright and there are lots of options.

Thank You

www.ingramcontent.com/pod-product-compliance
Lightning Source LLC
Chambersburg PA
CBHW080215170726
48282CB00030B/1122
9788119177936